Teleworking

A Guide to Good Practice

Alastair Reid

NCC Blackwell

MANCHESTER • OXFORD

First published 1994

First published in USA 1995

Blackwell Publishers
108 Cowley Road
Oxford OX4 1JF
UK

238 Main Street
Cambridge, Massachusetts 02142
USA

British Library Cataloguing in Publication Data

Reid, Alastair
  Teleworking – A Guide to Good Practice
  I. Title
  004.6

ISBN 1–85554–326–5

Library of Congress data is available

Typeset in 11 on 13pt Times Roman by H&H Graphics, Blackburn
Printed in Great Britain by Page Bros, Norwich.

This book is printed on acid-free paper

Contents

Nomenclature

Throughout this book a consistent style of computer nomenclature has been used. 'Personal computer' refers to all types and brands of personal computer. 'IBM PC' or 'PC' refers to personal computers compatible with the original IBM XT personal computer and its derivatives. Apple, Apple Mac and Macintosh refer to products of Apple Computer Inc. Acorn and Acorn/Archimedes refer to personal computers produced by Acorn Computers Limited.

Acknowledgements

My thanks are due to the many friends and colleagues who, wittingly and unwittingly, made invaluable contributions to this book. Thanks are due also to the many Telecottage Managers who provided copious information about their operations. Special thanks go to Alan Denbigh of ACRE for his suggestion to devote an entire chapter to the marketing and selling of Teleworked services.

Final thanks must go to my family for putting up with my more than usually irascible behaviour during the writing of this book. I am reliably informed that writing a book is the nearest a male comes to experiencing childbirth.

Preface

No one knows when the first teleworker started teleworking. He or she almost certainly did not realise at the time the breakthrough they were making. My own guess is that a lazy journalist writing a report of an event sitting comfortably in the office while listening to a radio commentary of that event, made that first small step.

No self-respecting journalist would approve of such a laissez-faire approach. It does however illustrate an important point. While this book is devoted almost entirely to considering teleworking using a personal computer and telephonic links, the nature of teleworking is limited only by one's vision and the ever-increasing capabilities of teleworking. Microwaves, satellites, television and radio are already being used in one form or another and current developments in what is known as "multi-media" will expand our horizons even further.

While the personal or 'micro' computer is the cornerstone of the teleworking concept, this is not a book for the computer buff. On the one hand, it seeks to demonstrate that teleworking is an environmentally friendly way for many enterprises to improve their performance, to further hone their competitive edge. On the other, it shows how teleworking can play a crucial role in re-vitalising remote rural communities by negotiating most of their geographic disadvantages.

Teleworking is not an economic panacea. However, in a world of increasing economic, political and environmental pressure, it has a considerable part to play. Most of the technology is readily available. The nature of that role is only limited by humanity's ingenuity and imagination.

This book dos not try to provide solutions . Rather, it seeks to make people fundamentally review their current work practices or, perhaps, the lack of them, with a view to improving the enterprises for which they work, the areas in which they live and, last but not least, their own aspirations and lifestyles.

Alastair Reid
Wigtown, October 1993

1 An Introduction to Teleworking

INTRODUCTION

'Teleworking' and 'telecommuting' are by now the two most widely accepted words to describe the whole range of work activities which are characterised by being carried out remotely from the normal expected place of work. Numerous other expressions such as homeworking and networking have been coined to describe it. For the purposes of clarity, Teleworking will be used throughout this text.

The work carried out usually involves the electronic processing of data although this may not be evident to the employer and worker, or the worker and his client. Both the supply of work and its output are carried between the employer and the worker or the worker and client via a telecommunication link, usually a telephone line.

Media interest in the concept of teleworking started in the early seventies. Prompted by the first oil crisis, a number of workers, notably Jack Nilles of the University of Southern California (1), suggested that the then infant science of Information Technology (IT) had the potential to substitute electronic communication for physical travel. In this instance, pressure to conserve oil, in the form of petrol, forced the scientists to think in an innovative way, and undoubtedly hastened the development of a powerful new technology.

A much more recent upsurge in one facet of teleworking occurred during the build up to and aftermath of, the Gulf War. During this period, there was a dramatic rise in demand for tele- or video-conferencing facilities. This demand was created not from the need to save jet fuel but from the widely perceived belief that civil aviation was going to be subjected to a wave of terrorist attacks. Those fears turned out to be unfounded, but many companies found that with video-conferencing they could make substantial savings in travel costs without sacrificing their operating efficiency.

Current estimates of the number of teleworkers in Britain vary wildly; from around 100,000 to one recent estimate from the Henley Centre for Forecasting of 1.5 million, a figure they expect to rise to 5 million by 1995. Computer industry watchers think these latter figures over-optimistic, and include people who now and again put a floppy disk in the post. At the present time (Autumn 1992) half a million seems a realistic estimate. For the purposes of this book 'Teleworkers' are people working either at home or in a small 'out-office' who receive and dispatch their work by wholly electronic means.

So who are these teleworkers? Most are self-employed, journalists, computer programmers, graphic designers, business consultants and the like. A much smaller number are employed by a few new companies which were set up specifically to exploit the teleworking concept. Very few are employed by large companies. BT, who clearly have a vested interest here, have been at the forefront of the corporate teleworking approach and recently launched a pilot scheme around the town of Inverness, with ten of their directory enquiry operators working directly from home. As well as a conventional computer link, they also have a special video-telephone link to their base to lessen the impact of isolation.

Without doubt teleworking could not have happened without the invention, development and subsequent explosive growth of the personal computer. Consequently, for those who are interested, a brief history of the electronic computer is given in Appendix 1.

As might be expected, developments in teleworking in Europe have been much more disjointed than in the USA, with little concerted action at national or regional level. The Commission of the European Communities has over the last couple of years taken the concept of teleworking very close to its heart, particularly with regard to its potential in disadvantaged areas, and has put its not inconsiderable weight behind it through its Opportunities for Rural Areas (ORA) scheme. However this initiative is already well bogged down in pan-European bureaucracy; it has produced a whole raft of projects and studies with acronyms such as ARTISAN, CORD, MITRE, RUDA and VERA, but so far, few enterprises actually running and practising teleworking have appeared on the ground.

A basic flaw in many of the ORA approaches is they are promoting teleworking from the bottom up rather than from the top down. Marketing strategies are being adopted whereby likely companies will be contacted to see if they could or would use the services of teleworkers. This assumes that the companies are not only aware of teleworking but more importantly, that the company has fully grasped what its administration side, and in many cases the entire enterprise, is trying to do.

An 'office' is a processing unit for information, no more and no less. The fact that today we now have the electronic if not the paperless office does not change that fundamental dictum. An enterprise's managers rely on information; information about costs, sales, markets, trends, customers, research, employees, exchange rates and so forth. This need, how it can be met and its impact on a business is dealt fully in Chapter 2 on Information Technology and Teleworking.

Proponents of teleworking, of which the author is obviously one, clearly believe that its advantages outweigh its disadvantages. However, it is important to realise that teleworking is not an economic or social panacea. It is obviously inappropriate in any functions that depend on face to face contact or personal attention such as receptionists and nurses. Nor will machine tool or production line operatives be able to telework. Other occupations still remain under threat from continuing automation. For example, bank tellers are being replaced by automatic cash dispensers. Some people still have to maintain the systems that support the dispensers and load them with cash but the change represents a fundamental shift in numbers and skills.

It is also important to appreciate that the large scale adoption of teleworking will have a far-ranging socio-economic impact. Consider for example, the effect on future road and rail development in the South East of England if forty percent of the employees in the financial institutions of the City of London were teleworking at home or at 'out–offices' much nearer their homes. Teleworking is unlikely to make quite such an impact on our work patterns but the wider socio-economic implications have to be taken on board at an early date.

THE ADVANTAGES OF TELEWORKING

Teleworking has advantages for the employer or corporate entity, the employee or individual, and the environment. It can provide new job opportunities for some of the disabled, mitigating some of the effects of immobility.

For most companies and organisations, teleworking will offer several advantages. Obvious ones are cost reduction, increased productivity and employee morale but there are many more less obvious, such as improved customer service and organisational flexibility. The introduction of teleworking can be, and some would go so far as to say should be, the cause for a fundamental re-appraisal of an organisation's or enterprise's basic management structure.

Cost savings can be achieved in a number of ways. Office overheads are usually second only to salaries as a fixed cost. Teleworking can remove the need to move to larger premises or offer the opportunity to move to a less expensive location. Even companies who insist on maintaining a 'prestige' head office can save by sub-letting superfluous parts of their premises. On the other hand, those still desirous of creating the right impression could find that teleworking enables them to consider smaller and more affordable premises than they had hitherto thought possible.

Teleworking can increase productivity in a variety of ways. One study (2) quotes increases of between 30 – 100 percent although it does not state how these increases were achieved. It is widely agreed that teleworkers are more productive than office-bound staff. The removal of the stress and strain of commuting is a major factor which in turn can give the individual a wider choice of housing. This can in turn help to reduce personal financial pressures (we live here because of John's work), as well as offering the teleworker a more attractive environment in which to live. Teleworkers usually have more hours available into which their work may be allocated, giving flexibility to both them and their employer. The combination of these and other factors means that teleworkers tend to be happier, appreciate the greater responsibility that teleworking entails and consequently tend to be highly motivated.

Changing demographic patterns in our population are placing increasing pressure on some areas of the labour market. Recruiting, training and retraining is, for many businesses becoming more and more difficult. Teleworking can at least ameliorate this problem in several ways. There will be less staff turnover from a responsible, highly motivated workforce enjoying a flexible approach to work as well as a better lifestyle. The same factors will help find and retain the right quality of staff with the additional bonus that the search can be extended far beyond the normal commuting area. A further benefit of teleworking is that it offers a novel way round a perennial problem with key female staff, maternity leave.

The concept of teleworking can offer an enterprise other advantages, especially to those whose businesses are more customer orientated. Helpline services can be dispersed and made more local as can telesales personnel, saving clients or potential customers expensive long-distance phone calls. Service engineers can be regarded as potential 'hybrid' teleworkers, living and working in their area, but teleworking from home for instruction, reporting or receiving specialist technical support. The efficiency of marketing and sales management departments should be analysed; would they be more effective if they were located out in the field rather than based at head office?

For most employees, the greatest benefit from teleworking will be the savings, mental as well as financial, from the ravages of daily commuting. Many will flourish in a new atmosphere of responsibility coupled with flexibility. Others, with caring responsibilities for either the young or the old and infirm will find teleworking an enormous help, enabling them to retain their role as provider while enhancing their ability to care, with a considerable reduction in mental wear and tear.

Perhaps the greatest individual benefits of teleworking will be to those living in either remote run-down or economically rundown communities. Teleworking can offer work opportunities without having to tear up one's roots, to the obvious advantage of the communities concerned. It is a change that will not happen overnight but already much is happening, and in many places the first green shoots are, as they say, beginning to show through. This book seeks to show how more of these seeds may be sown and their fruits successfully harvested.

It has often been said that the advent of the personal computer coupled with working from home will greatly benefit the disabled. This is perfectly true and most of us would probably think that teleworking is 'tailor-made' for the disabled. It is, but only up to a point. First, one has to be specific. The 'able' all too often use the word disabled very loosely, without thinking that there are many categories of disability, and that some of them are not even readily discerned by the casual observer.

To those whose disability affects their mobility, and they are not necessarily paraplegic, teleworking can be a marvellous window of opportunity. Commuting for them is not just difficult but often takes such a physical toll as to seriously lower their performance once they reach the workplace. But there is another side to the coin. Some of the disabled themselves actively regard teleworking as retrogressive (3), a return to the bad old days of keeping the disabled out of sight, and of course, out of mind. It is very, very hard for the able-bodied to understand how much pain and discomfort the disabled will tolerate just to experience the kaleidoscope of human contact that we all take for granted.

Nevertheless, the continued spread and acceptance of teleworking will be greeted with considerable enthusiasm by many of the disabled. Some vociferous opposition should not be allowed to subjugate the needs of a significant but silent minority. In particular it offers hope to the completely housebound and to others scope for less menial and more intellectually stimulating employment. No disability should ever be mistaken for lack of intellect.

While teleworking is generally regarded as a 'green' activity, its environmental impact is unlikely to be as great as one might think. B.T's extensive report (4) on the subject concludes that teleworking will be only slightly positive as far the overall UK energy balance is concerned. The most obvious potential environmental impact will be a reduction in urban commuting, taking pressure off congested city centres and overstretched public transport.

In the country, teleworking's effects will be more difficult to assess. It clearly offers hope to rural communities, but we have already seen in the past few years that rural society is every bit as fragile as the rural ecology. Several parts of Scotland and Wales have already suffered from an influx of 'white settlers' moving in from the affluent South East. On the one hand they force property prices up and out of reach of the young local population. On the other, they fiercely resist any form of 'progress' which might disturb their rural idyll, thus depriving the indigenous population of any opportunity for economic betterment. A judicious leavening of the population with some high earning and spending teleworkers will certainly help rural economies, but a large scale invasion certainly would not.

THE DISADVANTAGES OF TELEWORKING

Corporate reservations about teleworking centre mainly on the control and management of teleworkers, the terms and conditions of employment, and, depending on the nature of the enterprise, commercial security. For the employee and the individual, the downside of teleworking is the potential loss status, and coping with the alternating pressures of family life and professional isolation.

Traditional methods of management have depended very much on the 'over the shoulder' type of supervision and this clearly is inappropriate for teleworking. The simplest approach is to measure performance sole on the quality of the output, without paying too much attention as to how or when the work was done. This will be adequate for some types of work but such laissez faire attitudes do not rest lightly on corporate shoulders. The Stanworths (5) say that the type and nature of remote supervision of the teleworker will be affected by:

- the nature of the work;

- the status and knowledge of the teleworker;

- the organisational culture and tradition.

This will require a considerable change in management attitudes in many organisations and will in all probability lead to the development and introduction of new management techniques to deal with what might be called 'Wide Area Management'.

Contractual arrangements for teleworkers will have to strike a careful balance. They must ensure on the one hand that the regular office staff do not feel that the teleworker is getting preferential or kid-glove treatment. On the other, teleworkers have to feel that they are not being exploited or are in any way inferior to conventional employees.

A further corporate concern can be the effect of teleworking scattering the workforce and thus dilute morale or erode the corporate culture. This may not be so much of a problem when a person becomes a teleworker after a period of working for a company in a conventional way, and be familiar with its house style and management methods. For a raw recruit, unfamiliar with company practices, personnel departments may well have to put together a teleworker's starter-pack and institute schemes both to monitor teleworker performance and morale as well as keep them up to date with company news and developments. Teleworker social evenings could be run in various locales if numbers justify such an approach.

With regard to security, a teleworker's home will be less secure than a company office, both in regard to burglar protection as well as the presence of unauthorised visitors. Strict protocols will have to be adopted for all teleworkers, in particular those handling sensitive personal and corporate information. These will have to cover computer and network access, document and electronic record protection against both fire and theft as well as control of any paper waste.

For the individual, the disadvantages of being a teleworker are predominately psychological. Loss of status, apparent lack of security, the effects of isolation and increased domestic pressure have already been well documented, and teleworking is still in its infancy.

Perceived loss of status can be a major problem for some individuals both inside and outside the workplace. If enforced, teleworking can be seen by some as a sort of half-way house to redundancy, to others, the loss of the trappings of office life or being shunted out of the centre of activity will be regarded at best as a corporate slap in the face. People harbouring such grudges are unlikely to be successful teleworkers. Enforced teleworking will have to be handled with great sensitivity if it is to be successfully implemented. Not everyone will regard it as progressive and some will be frightened by the new self-discipline being thrust upon them.

The status problem can also manifest itself socially, in the town, in the pub or just amongst friends. Some still regard working from home as a soft option, and to the managerial classes, consultancy has become a euphemism for being unemployed. Each of these can lead to a build-up of personal and family tensions which can seriously affect a teleworker's performance and this new area of industrial psychology merits serious academic study.

The question of isolation is more difficult. It is well known that many people, women in particular, go to work solely for the social interaction of the workplace, and remuneration is very much a fringe benefit. Removed from the gossip and intrigue of the average office some will find that a job is no longer worthwhile. Some others will retreat further into their protective shells and venture out of their homes less often than they do at present. Neither type is likely to make a good teleworker.

For the teleworker, home is the workplace, and the home is of course the source of many other social pressures. A teleworker does not have the option of going off to work in the morning to get away from any domestic trouble he or she may be afflicted with, and as yet there are no easy answers to this one. Teleworking is unlikely to be the saviour of a faltering marriage. The necessity of wholehearted family support for the teleworker is more fully dealt with in Chapter 6.

WHO CAN BE A TELEWORKER?

A number of writers have attempted to define the nature of jobs which can be teleworked and drawn up lists of specific job titles or categories of job titles. Others use phrases such as 'information intensive' or 'knowledge based' to classify teleworking jobs. The danger of producing long lists of suitable teleworking applications is that they might inhibit the creation of some innovative new applications. This book tries to use a more open approach and while it does provide an illustrative list of suitable activities, it also endeavours to enunciate the basic principles and capabilities of teleworking.

Modern technology, through the personal computer, the modem and the fax machine means that large amounts of information which can be converted into what is known as a 'digital' format can be moved long distances at considerable speed using the telephone lines. Notable exceptions to this are noise, be it music or the human voice and moving pictures. The latter may seem extraordinary given that we receive our television pictures through a simple co-axial cable. Suffice it to say that the technology is quite different. A more readily understood analogy is that a Compact Disc can hold about one hour of music but an identical disk in a computer's read only memory can hold around 250,000 typed A4 pages of information.

In essence computers manipulate pieces of information. While the computer only understands a weird form of numbers known as the binary system, computer programmers have devised ways in which text, numbers, lines, in fact every single spot or pixel on the computer's screen can be represented by these binary numbers, or digitised and can then be juggled about by the computer according to various instructions. We know these sets of instructions as computer programs or software, and Chapter 8 is devoted to describing the different types of software available.

Not everyone who spends their working day sitting in front of a computer terminal can be a teleworker. The crucial element is how the information being processed by the computer operator is presented to them. In almost every case in every organisation it will be on paper and one then has to consider how and where was that paper generated and by whom. Periodic announcements regarding the imminent arrival of the paperless office have all been premature. Inspite of widespread computerisation (perhaps even because of it) 95 percent of business information is still held in paper form. One explanation for this is that so much information is in a form that does not lend itself to the computing arena, such as handwritten notes and forms, typewritten letters and reports. Then, of course there are these enormous computer print-outs. A more likely, but seemingly unrecognised explanation, is that the vast majority of people are far more efficient and comfortable assimilating information from a piece of paper than they are from a computer's monitor.

There are three main categories here; paper generated within the organisation, paper from outside the organisation and paper with which the organisation communicates to the outside world. Good organisational analysis and appropriate use of computers, large and small can minimise the first of these, but theory and plain common sense must always ensure that whatever system or procedures are adopted, they *really* meet the needs of the enterprise and are not merely 'making a statement' about the organisation. It must always be horses for courses; for example, many small retail operations will benefit more from a sophisticated cash register than from a personal computer and an accounting package.

To cope with what can be a continuous avalanche of incoming paper, help is at hand in the shape of a relatively new technology, Document Image Processing, DIP. At its simplest, DIP involves the electronic 'scanning' of any piece of paper and its conversion into a digital record which can then be manipulated, transported and viewed electronically. DIP and its application, Image Management Systems IMS, is thought by many IT gurus to be the 'in' technology of the nineties. Already some far-sighted companies routinely have all their incoming mail scanned and then electronically distributed to its recipients. Some believe DIP has the potential to eliminate up to 50 percent of the paper used in business, others that the European market for IMS and its associated hardware will be in excess of three billion dollars by 1995. Since that would represent a compound annual growth rate of

62 percent since 1990, it would appear to be an overly ambitious prediction.

While one can argue about the rate of introduction of DIP and IMS, what is not in doubt is that it represents an entirely new window of opportunity for teleworking. A major stumbling block to the adoption of teleworking to data-inputting tasks is that the raw data comes in the form of paper, delivery notes, invoices, application forms and the like and these are normally delivered by mail or handed in to either a branch or head office. DIP and IMS can now provide the means for all that paperwork to be electronically distributed to the operators processing the data, thus eliminating the need for vast single offices areas and all of the associated expense.

Most employers have given little thought to the concept of teleworking and consequently have little or no perception of what teleworking can do for their organisation or even which jobs are suitable for teleworking. Olson (6) identified six criteria which should be met for jobs to be suitable for teleworking.

- have a high thought rather than manual labour content;
- work that is carried out by individuals, not teams:
- can be done with minimal supervision, any initiative being vested in the worker;
- output is readily measurable;
- success of performance is readily measurable;
- does not require expensive or bulky capital equipment.

The Stanworths (5) produced a selection of activities which lend themselves which they divided into five level of what one might call management seniority:

1 *Professionals and Management Specialists:* Architects, accountants, corporate finance, design engineers, financial analysts, graphic designers, general managers, public relations, educationalists, translators.

2 *Professional support workers:* Bookkeepers, desktop publishing, draughtsmen, indexers, information retrieval, literature searchers, proof-readers, researchers, technical support staff.

3 *'Itinerant' field workers:* Auditors, company sales representatives, inspectors, insurance brokers, property negotiators, schools inspectors, service engineers, surveyors.

4 *Information Technology Specialists:* Systems analysts, software programmers, systems engineers.

5 Clerical Support Workers: Data entry staff, directory enquiry staff, secretarial staff, telesales staff, word processor operators.

The above lists are by no means comprehensive but should give an idea of the tremendous breadth of opportunity teleworking can offer, both to the individual and to the enterprise. It can, when intelligently implemented, offer the irresistible combination of a better service or function for less money.

OPPORTUNITIES IN TELEWORKING

As well as offering the wide range of job opportunities outlined above, the last few years have seen the emergence of some new kinds of company who owe their very existence to the teleworking concept. These companies were set up by a number of far-sighted entrepreneurs who saw, in some cases before the very word teleworking was coined, that the combination of the personal computer, the modem and the telephone network, could fulfil a number of market opportunities. In some cases the driving force was a social need, in others, a way of harnessing a scarce human resource in an innovative way.

The F.I. Group plc was founded in 1962 by Mrs Steve Shirley and has been a pioneer of homeworking in the computer industry. Mrs Shirley set up the F.I. company as a form of emancipation and most of the early team were, like Mrs Shirley, women who were experienced computer programmers and now confined to the house with the responsibility of a growing family. F.I. now employs about 1,000 professional programmers, the majority of whom are female and who either work at home or in a number of drop-in work centres scattered around the country.

Crossaig Ltd., based in Helensburgh, Scotland was set up by Huw Baynham to provide a rapid editing service for English language medical articles. The summaries are fed into the 'Embase' on-line database run by the Dutch publishing company, Elsevier Science Publishing. The editing process requires editors with scarce medical and scientific skills and teleworking enables Crossaig to use editors living throughout Scotland. The editors are connected to Crossaig's office by ISDN links and a PC. According to Baynham, the ISDN link eliminates the need for the widely scattered editors to regularly meet at a central location which would be very impractical.

Crossaig has also found that teleworking has reduced the time required to edit medical journals from four weeks to just one. This rapid turnaround means that Embase has accurate and concise reviews of the latest medical developments within days, and often ahead of competing databases, giving them a significant competitive advantage.

Telesec of Brighton has used teleworking to provide an novel alternative to the office temp. Telesec offer a bureau secretarial service using teleworkers working from their own homes. Telesec usually receive their work by fax which is then sent on to a teleworker, again by fax. The completed document file is then sent back to the Telesec office where hard copy can be produced and couriered to the client or electronically transmitted for the client to print out on his own headed paper. Telesec boast a turnround time of four hours and point out that since the work is costed on a 'per page' basis, it can be much cheaper than employing an under-utilised temp, paid by the day or half-day. Telesec's services are used by self-employed executives working from home who need occasional secretarial support as well as companies needing extra secretarial capacity.

In what are still the formative years of teleworking, a number of as yet unexploited opportunities spring to mind. There is clearly scope for teleworking bureaux who will have a database of teleworkers with a variety of skills for short and long term hire. No recruitment agencies specialising in teleworking have yet appeared to tap what promises to be a lucrative field of activity in the not-too-distant future. There will also be opportunities for on-line distance training and learning, either for computer training itself or in appropriate school and college subjects.

There will also be scope for information retrieval services as companies start to 'privatise' these and other such activities and concentrate on their core activities. Some companies may go so far as to use third party providers to maintain and update their Executive Information Systems, EIS. There will also be growth in industry or profession specific literature survey services analogous to that provided by Crossaig. Teleworking on the grand scale is already being practised by the national newspapers and there is surely scope for a teleworking enterprise using Desktop Publishing (DTP) to specialise in the production of company newsheets or 'house' newspapers.

These spin-offs will not be restricted to industry; continuing drives for efficiency in government, both local and national, as well as in the newly created NHS trusts offer a wealth of opportunity for the farsighted and innovative teleworker.

THE DATA INDUSTRY

At this stage, when considering the opportunities for teleworking, it is appropriate to introduce the reader to some of the mysteries of the Data Industry. While almost everyone has been aware of the extraordinary growth in the computer industry over the past decade, the parallel development and growth of the data or information industry has been almost furtive by comparison.

The progressive realisation that information was the life blood of any enterprise was touched on at the beginning of this chapter. Yet all too many British enterprises have so far failed to take this fundamental commercial dictum on board. Its impact can be far-reaching. Our own British Telecom and a few other far sighted PTT's transformed themselves when they realised that they were not in the telephone business but were in fact in the information transmission business.

To the prospective teleworker, this means that vast amounts of information, from the general to the highly technical and specific, can be accessed through an on-line database. It has been estimated that there are about 5,000 publicly accessible databases world-wide, of which around 500 are based in Britain. Only a few on-line databases are free of charge, the Electronic Yellow Pages being a notable example. Most charge by the minute for access and this is in addition to the charges you will be running up on the phone line. Nevertheless, this can represent good value when compared with the cost of sending someone to wade through the local (if there is one) commercial library. One enterprising teleworker has already set up his own specialised company based at his home which carries out company searches on request and faxes the output to the client.

A basic insight into what an on-line database looks like can be gained by looking at the teletext services provided by the BBC and ITV. Known as Ceefax and Oracle, they give a broad indication of how an on-line database is structured and what it can contain. As a matter of interest, plug-in cards for personal computers are available, which, when connected to a TV antenna gives a teletext capability to a computer. Such cards cost around £200 and some people may find it a cheaper alternative to buying a teletext TV set.

The range and detail held on these on-line databases is quite extraordinary. On the one hand there are straightforward retrieval systems which will list all articles in a selected newspaper or magazine containing a particular keyword. Others are highly specific databases covering a vast range of specialised subjects from Artificial Intelligence Abstracts through the Martindale Pharmacopoeia to Zoological Records On-line.

While there are some exceptions such as Reuter's 'On Demand', Kompass On-line and ICC Information Services, the vast majority of on-line databases are accessed through what is known as a 'host' computer service. In Britain the most prominent of these services are provided by 'FT Profile', 'DataStar', 'Dialog' and the 'Manchester Host Computer' .

FT Profile

FT Profile is the Financial Times' on-line information service. It gives users instant access to a wide range of information from newspapers and business publishers. Material from over 2,000 international publications and information services dating back several years is stored on a large database. Users can connect to the service directly or through a local PSS number.

Datastar

Datastar is the British brand of a number of on-line database services run by Radio Suisse. Datastar was set up in 1981 and offers over 250 databases with world-wide coverage although the emphasis is on Europe. The main areas covered include business news, statistics and analysis, healthcare and pharmaceuticals, chemicals and petrochemicals, biomedicine and the sciences, bio-technology and technology. 'Focus' is an easy-to-use menu driven service giving access to Datastar's most important databases. 'Tradstat' is the world's largest trade statistics service. All the Radio Suisse on-line services can be accessed through the PSS network.

Dialog

Dialog is an American based on-line database service. The service has been operating since 1972 and has over 400 databases containing in excess of 300 million records. Dialog also runs a full text service for over 1, 600 international technical and specialist publications. Once again Dialog can be entered via the PSS network.

Manchester Host Computer

The Manchester Host computer service, launched in March 1991, is the result of a unique initiative by Manchester City Council. With funding from the Department of the Environment's Urban Programme the Council formed a partnership with Soft Solutions Limited, an established player in the data industry. It will appeal to many prospective teleworkers as it operates a user-friendly menu system called 'find' and is relatively inexpensive with charges varying from £0.25 to £1.50 per minute (excluding call charges). The Manchester Host service offers access to more than 150 on-line databases grouped under eight main headings:

- Environment, Health & Safety
- Business & Finance
- People & Society
- News & Travel
- Science, Technology, Agriculture
- Local Information (N.W. England)
- Europe
- Government, Law, Planning.

As well as operating as an access point to on-line databases, the Manchester Host also offers a number of related telecommunication services such as electronic mail, fax and telex, file transfer and bulletin boards. It also publishes for subscribers a most informative monthly newsletter *'Manchester On-Line'*.

Scottish services

For prospective teleworkers living in Scotland, the Network Service Agency based in Inverness offer the NSA-Host service as well as a less complex International Research and Information Service, IRIS-ONLINE. NSA enjoys the support and technical backup of its parent company, British Telecom. These services offer connectivity to both Apple Mac and IBM PCs. As well as operating an information host system, the NSA also offers electronic mail and electronic conferencing services.

Contact telephone numbers for all the services mentioned above can be found in Appendix 2.

At this point the Data Industry with its plethora of information contained in this huge range of on-line databases probably remains a mystery to most readers. Collectively, however, they probably represent the greatest single work opportunity to the prospective teleworker. Whether in gathering and collating information to go on to databases as with Crossaig (q.v.) or in extracting and editing information for presentation to clients in readily assimilated form; the scope is almost boundless. It is up to the individual to identify these opportunities and convert them to a successful commercial enterprise.

The introduction to this book stated that the scope of teleworking was largely limited by humanity's ingenuity and imagination. It is to be hoped that this section has given readers plenty of food for thought.

START-UP COSTS

Fortunately for the prospective teleworker, prices of personal computers in general and PCs in particular are falling at a remarkable rate at the present time and processing power has never been cheaper. The average price of a powerful 486DX PC has fallen over 35 percent in the year to October 1992. The reductions that have been seen throughout the past year cannot go on for ever and a number of smaller computer assemblers have succumbed to the recession. As a result, there has never been a better time to buy a personal computer and consequently the start-up costs for the teleworker have never been more advantageous.

As will be explained later in this book, one should only choose a computer once you have decided what you want it to do and selected the software for that task. Then you select a computer to run the chosen software. To complicate matters, there are several types of personal computer and the first essential is to ensure that you choose one that will be fully compatible with your employer or prospective client. In the UK, three types dominate the business market, the IBM PC and its look-alikes, the Apple Macintosh and the Acorn/Archimedes.

The IBM PC and its clones dominate the business market. The Apple Macintosh has similar domination in the fields of graphics and publishing, but is relatively uncommon in business. The Acorn/Archimedes is widely used in schools and education, although Apple are making significant inroads to this sector. While there is now some cross-platform connectivity between these three types, it is essential that you carefully select the same type as your employer or client or that is predominant in your chosen speciality.

Within these three categories there is a considerable range of computing power available for an equally wide range of prices. Detailed examination of the varieties of software and hardware that are available comes later in this book, in Chapters 7 and 8 respectively. Information on selection and purchasing procedures are given in Chapter 9. However, at this early stage it does not seem unreasonable to give some broad indications of start-up costs. Without getting bogged down in detail, and to give a broad indication of the range of costs involved, we shall consider three different levels of PC, basic, median and power user. Details of the technical specification of each of these three computers are given in Chapter 8. All prices are what might be described as 'on-the-street' and include VAT.

1. Basic System:

386SX-25MHz., 2Mb RAM, l00Mb hard disk,

Bubble-jet printer

Modem

Fax machine

Dedicated phone line

Suite of software

2. Median System:

486DX-33MHz., 8Mb RAM, 210Mb hard disk

Laser printer

Modem

Fax machine

Dedicated phone line

Suite of software

3. Power User:

486DX-66MHz, 16Mb RAM, 340Mb hard disk

17" monitor

"Postscript" laser printer

ISDN card

ISDN 2 line connection

Suite of software

It does not seem appropriate in a book that will be read in many different countries to quote even guide prices in any specific currency. Thus a Median System will cost about 1.5 times that of the base system while a 'Power' system will be about 2.5 times more expensive. Readers should note that in each of these three systems the cost of the computer itself is less than 30 percent of the cost of the complete system. This is frequently overlooked when people first get involved in personal computing. In each of the above examples, the suite of software is assumed to have cost the same as the computer itself. A personal computer is nothing without its software and peripherals.

It must be emphasised that the above are no more than broad price guides and there is scope to both increase and reduce them according to personal and professional requirements. The above estimates do not take account of any office furniture that may be required by the prospective teleworker since price variations here are huge and are entirely a matter of personal taste as well as one's budget.

2 Information Technology and Teleworking

INTRODUCTION

Information Technology or IT as it is more commonly known, is certainly one of managements' 'buzzwords' of the eighties and nineties. We have all see the advertisements in the 'sits vac' sections of the heavier newspapers, *IT Professionals*, *Multi- disciplined IT Director* and so on, couched in the wordy mumbo jumbo so beloved of the recruitment company copywriters.

The concept of teleworking is a direct descendent of IT.

But just what is IT? Can it readily be defined? A reasonable definition from the PA Consulting Group (7) goes as follows:

In the broadest sense IT is about computers and communications. More specifically IT deals with systems that capture, transmit, process, store and retrieve information. With proper management it can magnify the talent and skills of a company's staff and open new areas of business. If not properly controlled, it can mis-direct corporate energy, waste valuable resources and damage a company's competitiveness.

The PA Consulting Group's book, whose main thrust is the need to adopt IT to meet the challenge of what is known as the single European market in 1992, goes on to refer to the work of Michael Porter of Harvard Business School (8) and (9) and the gradual realisation in academia that information is the lifeblood of an enterprise and without information the modern organisation is dead. This important concept was eagerly grasped by computer and systems analysts alike, who were quick to see it as a way of promoting themselves from being merely a service to an enterprise or organisation to being at the very heart of the decision making process.

A number of people, the EEC Commissioners among them, believe that it is necessary to have an indigenous IT industry before one can reap the benefits of IT, and to this end the Commission set up ESPRIT (European Strategic Programme for Research in Information Technology), a £2.1 billion collaborative programme. ESPRIT's objectives were to foster international cooperation within the Community, develop new technologies and to set pan-European IT standards. ESPRIT has had some success but the global IT supply industry continues to be dominated by IBM, Digital and Unisys in the USA and Fujitsu, NEC and Hitachi in Japan.

Does this matter? Yes, but only to the extent that the electronics industry will represent only a fraction of any country's Gross Domestic Product (GDP). In Britain for example, the major players have either been taken over by overseas interests or are the result of inward investment, hence the creation of silicon glen and silicon cwm. These so-called 'sunrise' industries play a vital role in the communities where they have been established, not least because they have largely replaced the traditional heavy industries such as coal, iron and steel in these areas. These days, be it motor cars or electronics, the brandname gives no clue as to the product's country of origin.

This book contends that the source of IT, be it the hardware or the know-how is of less importance to a nations' economic well-being, than the wholesale adoption of the technologies by the rest of its governing and commercial enterprises.

In concluding this introduction, and taking the above definition as a basis, the author has tried to come up with a more concise and accurate definition of IT:

Information Technology is an enabling technology, the use of computers and telecommunications is to provide the managers of an enterprise or organisation with the information necessary to enhance their performance and that of their enterprise or organisation.

THE BEGINNINGS OF INFORMATION TECHNOLOGY

In the good old days business information centred around the control of money and materials or resources which had a monetary value. Clerks perched on high stools entered details of every transaction into large books called ledgers. Even then, enterprises needed to know that the monies owing to them were paid, and conversely that they paid out the monies that they owed. These accounting procedures also had to ensure that tax regimes were met and that there was no theft or misuse of company funds or materials. Since most enterprises aim to make a profit, the profit and loss account became the most convenient way of assessing a business's performance.

The ledger is still the foundation of accounting practice today. The sales ledger indicates who owes the company money, the purchase ledger shows to whom the company owes money. The standard format of the ledger easily lends itself to computerisation, each ledger holding a 'record' for each transaction. These early programmes then progressed from simply holding records to manipulating them and in particular being able to automatically compute the extension and any tax requirements. Thus, if customer number 1234 ordered 2,500 mark 3 widgets, the system, knowing the unit price and the customer's rate of discount would automatically work out the extension and then calculate the VAT.

As well as providing very high accuracy in repetitious calculations, it was soon discovered that the computer's ability to sort data very rapidly could provide the company with a new kind of information, financial and quantitative analysis. It became possible to analyse sales trends as well as the costs of various centres of activity. Labour costs could be analysed to show which departments were more or less efficient. Payrolls themselves were frequently the first accounting function to be computerised, but there are widely differing views on the efficacy of computerisation for the payroll. Until quite recently one distinguished computer manufacturer's own payroll was calculated manually.

The creation of these increasingly complex computer systems was the responsibility of 'system managers'. Eventually in many large organisations this 'systems' function spawned a whole new department, often referred to as the data processing (DP) section. When DP grew up, it became IT. Whatever its title, the computer section had three main tasks. The first of these was system analysis. The analyst was the link between the user, sales, accounts, production, personnel and so on, and the service provider, the computer section. Analysts had to have a blend of practical business knowledge, the skill to assess the user's needs and an appreciation of the essential capabilities of the computer.

The second task was programming, the creation of the software which would meet the needs of the user. It has to be remembered here that we are still in the sixties and the seventies, dealing with mainframe and mini-computers and the days of pre-packed ready-to-run software were some way off. The programmer had to draw up a programme specification and then proceed to write the innumerable lines of code in the appropriate programming language. The new programme then had to be tested and all the mistakes and errors removed, a process known a 'debugging'. Once the new programme had been thoroughly tested and installed, it was then handed over to the third section of the computer division, 'operations'.

'Operations' task was to oversee the entry of data into the suite of programmes run by the organisation and supervise the running of the hardware itself. Depending on the complexity of the organisation, the operations section might be subdivided into smaller units with specific responsibilities such as computer operations, database administration, data entry, tape or disk librarian and so forth. This classical structure remained very much the same until the arrival of the personal computer introduced a whole new dimension to the world of data processing.

THE PERSONAL COMPUTER

The introduction of the first personal computers in the late seventies soon dispelled for ever the mystique that surrounded the mainframe computer and its acolytes. While the early personal computers were the playthings of the established computer freak, a number of far sighted entrepreneurs saw that there were tremendous commercial opportunities to be made in offering 'ready made' software packages to be used by this new generation of inexpensive computers. These software packages transformed what was a mysterious box of electronic wizardry to an office machine to help a secretary, accountant or manager. The software publishing industry had been born.

It is difficult to appreciate the impact of this fundamental change. For the first thirty odd years of the commercial computer virtually all the software was custom designed for each application, although it would be written in one of a number of standard 'languages'. Within a couple of years or so a wide range of software packages could be obtained off the shelf and the whole face of computing was changed for ever. A detailed treatment of personal computer software is given in Chapter 8.

Thus, the explosive growth in the use of personal computers was due less to the extraordinary power of the microchip than to the availability of a wide range of relatively inexpensive application programmes for wordprocessing, spreadsheets and databases. In fact it was the personal computer software publishers who were the rocket which pulled the personal computer manufacturers to stardom. While these software packages were promoted as being user friendly, few users ever progressed beyond learning the bare essentials. It has frequently been said that about 90 percent of software users use only 15 percent of the applications' capability. At worst, a personal computer can be a very expensive electric typewriter.

LOCAL AREA NETWORKS (LANS)

When the personal computer was in its infancy the business world was initially unconvinced and felt it had little use other than in a few specialist applications. This all changed with the advent of the network. Networks, known as LAN's (Local Area Network) resulted from the transfer of the multi-user concept to the personal computer.

LAN's come in three basic flavours; the 'Star' or 'Client-Server' type (Figure 2.1) the 'Bus' type (Figure 2.2) and the 'Ring' type (Figure 2.3).

DEVELOPMENT OF LANS

The development of the LAN spawned a whole new branch of the computer industry and the concept quickly grew in both size and complexity to meet the ever increasing demands of commerce. Small LANs could be connected to other or larger LANs by means switching equipment such as 'bridgers' which learns the addresses on each LAN and only forwards the relevant information from one network to the other, or 'routers' which can find the most effective route between two personal computers where several large LANs are linked together. Linking LANs together means that several hundred personal computers can directly communicate with each other and share information. An important downside of this progress is that the complex cabling and cable-ducting required by complex and multiple LANs has rendered many relatively new office buildings obsolete

The introduction of networks and networking transformed business

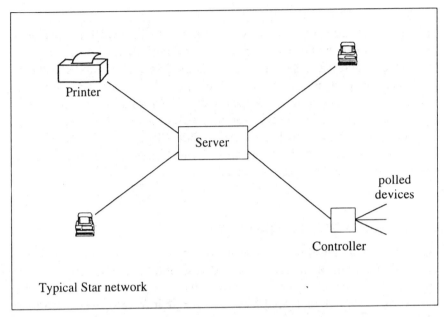

Figure 2.1   The Star or Client-server type LAN

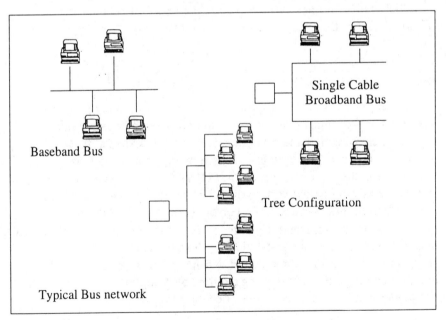

Figure 2.2   The 'Bus' type LAN

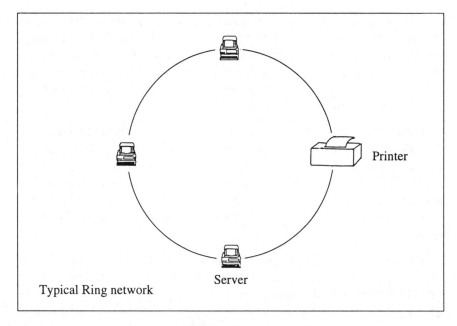

Printer

Server

Typical Ring network

Figure 2.3   The 'Ring' type LAN

attitudes to the personal computer. Suddenly, mainframe or mini-computing power was readily and cheaply available, and personal computer sales went into orbit.

WIDE AREA NETWORKS (WANS)

In the broad sense a WAN is a group of computers that are on the one hand physically separated by long distances and on the other logically and operationally tied together. The WAN has two main functions; to allow people who are physically separate to share common information, and to let them send information to each other. Unlike local area networks WANs do not have to be kept on-line at all times, this is only done when a private or rented communication network is available, as in the banking sector. All teleworkers are, at least some of the time, part of a WAN.

There are six widely used techniques for making the physical connection between computers and a further seven ways in which the connected computers can communicate. The connections appropriate for teleworkers will be either the normal telephone network or ISDN. The other more specialised methods are private or leased telephone lines, packet switched network such as X.25, and leased data transfer lines such as Kilostream and Megastream. A more detailed treatment of communication links, modems and communication software is given in Chapter 5.

The simplest and commonest form of computer communication over a distance is by direct modem-to-modem file transfer and this is what is used by the vast majority of teleworkers. The three most important factors in configuring a WAN are speed, speed and speed. It is important to appreciate how slow data transfer is over a remote connection compared with the rates of data transfer within a personal computer. This is shown in Table 2.1 below.

The above table should put into perspective the huge gap between relative data transfer speeds of even the most advanced telecommunication link and the transfer rates inside a personal computer. Modem rates do not present great problems when transferring text-only files but can become less

Table 2.1   Comparison of data

Remote Connections		Local Connections	
2400 bps modem	240 cps	Floppy disk	44,000 cps
9600 bps V.32 modem	960 cps	Ethernet LAN	1,000,000 cps
64,000 bps ISDN	6,400 cps	ESDI hard disk	1,600,000 cps
1.5 Mbps leased digital line	150,000 cps	33MHz 386 talking to RAM	66,000,000 cps

cps = Characters per second

practical and more expensive when dealing with graphical files which by their nature are very much larger.

While prospective teleworkers do not need to get bogged down in the technicalities of WAN s, they should at least familiarise themselves with the basic principles involved, if only to help them sell a service that will be delivered by teleworking. First, they need to know to what the proposed connection will be made, to another personal computer, a Local Area Network (LAN) or a mini or mainframe computer. Next, they need to consider the nature of the data that will be transferred over the WAN; is it simply file transfer or will there have to be on-line connections with the ability to transfer control of the LAN to a remote site? If so, what are the security implications?

A large number of specialist texts on Local Area Networks and Wide Area Networks are available for those who wish to learn more about this complex subject.

Important variations of Wide Area Networks are Bulletin Board Services and E-Mail Services. Single user Bulletin Board Services, BBS, are not so common in Britain as in the USA. The BBS is a computer running unattended and is called by the user either to upload or download files or messages addressed to other users. E-mail services are similar to BBS but operate on a wide scale using local nodes of a packet switched network (PSS) such as Dialplus.

Summarising, the WAN is the method by which the teleworker is connected to the outside world, be it client, employer or information source.

DOWNSIZING

'Downsizing' usually refers to the replacement of a mainframe or mini-computer with a Local Area Network (LAN), of personal computers. Replacing a mainframe by a network of high performance personal computers is said to reduce capital and operational IT expenditure by over 50 percent, a claim that is not unnaturally disputed by the mainframe and mini-computer manufacturers.

However the arrival of the PC LAN or even interconnected LANs does not herald the imminent demise of the mainframe computer. The PC LAN will not, in the foreseeable future, be able to meet two crucial requirements of the large corporate mainframe user, viz. restart and recovery of multiple transactions and data integrity and security. Ordinary mortals will find it difficult to comprehend the sheer number crunching power of a modern mainframe computer, with a storage capacity measured not even in Giga-Bytes (1,000 MBytes) but Terra-Bytes, one million Mbytes! Rumours of the death of the mainframe are premature and greatly exaggerated.

What is more realistic, and already starting to happen, is the development of what are known as 'open' systems. Open systems are a new generation of computer operating systems which are recognised by, and can operate with a whole range of different CPUs. The ultimate objective, still some way off, is that personal computers, workstations, mini-computers and mainframes will have complete compatibility and be able to link together in a seamless manner. This will be of great benefit to growing businesses who will eventually be able to progress from a single PC to a PC LAN and via a mini-computer to a mainframe without any expensive changes in software and basic work practices.

Returning to 'downsizing', there is a great deal more to it than simply buying a number of personal computers. To be really effective, downsizing has to be accompanied by changes in both work and business practices, changes that can only be achieved after the most rigorous study of the organisation's current modus operandi.

This organisational rethink is absolutely vital. The worst possible strategy is to automate existing procedures. It is better by far to see if the procedures are really necessary. Why replace the office junior with a robot when the judicious use of a network and electronic mail would remove the need for an office junior altogether? In considering downsizing, as with every aspect of IT, the needs of the enterprise or organisation must override all other considerations and never become subservient to the capabilities of the technology.

Before considering the commercial impact of the personal computer and the further development of IT, we should first pause and consider some mainframe applications which have been of far-reaching importance. The first of these concerns Retailing and Electronic Point of Sales, the second Banking and Electronic Fund Transfer in its various forms and finally the newspaper industry, 'The Press'.

RETAILING

We are now all familiar with the bar codes that appear on everything from a tin of beans to a packet of crisps. The bar code is read by a laser gun, usually placed in a box beside the cash register at the check-out point. When an article with a bar code is read by passing it over the laser beam, a micro computer in the cash register causes the full details of the article and its price to be printed on the cash roll. Provision of an itemised receipt to the customer is just a fringe benefit as far as the store is concerned. This combination of a bar code reader and a cash register is known as an Electronic Point of Sale (EPOS). EPOS provides the store management with a continuous picture of the stock position of every article in the store and also the rate at which individual lines are being purchased. The system can automatically draw up its re-ordering requirements, while management can adjust new orders to cater for the changing purchasing patterns of the store's customers. For example, order levels will vary according to the day of the week.

Bar code reading systems can be configured in a number of ways. The commonest is for the cash registers and bar code readers to be permanently linked to a mini-computer in the store. This can either be continuously linked through a dedicated private telephone line to a mainframe at head office, or else upload its data at set times in the course of the day through a modem. Setting up an EPOS system is expensive with one of the supermarket chains being quoted as saying a nationwide system cost it around £65m. These high costs have been quickly offset by gains in operating efficiency and reduced labour costs, the goods no longer having to be individually priced before they are placed on the shelves.

EPOS is an extraordinarily powerful tool in retailing. It can almost instantly tell the store operator how various layout configurations affect sales and monitor individual product lines or overall sales on an hour by hour basis so the operator can optimise opening times. To the manufacturer of the whole gamut of products to be found in today's supermarkets, EPOS and the cooperation of the store operator can rapidly provide invaluable data on the consumer's reaction to a new pack design, different merchandising techniques or simply the effect of a change in price. Similarly, it can also provide much faster results from test marketing a new product than has been possible hitherto.

The big supermarket chains have clearly honed EPOS to something close to perfection as has been borne out by their financial results. In other sectors of retailing the results have been much more mixed, with the High Street witnessing some notable collapses and falls from grace. This clearly demonstrates that with Information Technology what matters most is the effective assimilation of the information, not its collection.

BANKING

The banking sector has been at the forefront of DP and IT since their inception. Yet the sector as a whole cannot be said to be entirely at ease with the new technology and recent results indicate a need for at least some of the clearing banks to go back to first principles.

Originally, banking involved bankers and their clients in face-to-face relationships and depended very much on the personal chemistry of those relationships. The entire profession was geared to this approach and, according to Smith and Wield (10), "the recruitment, pay, training and career assumptions which applied to bank staff were above all directed at maintaining a financially secure, dutiful, deferential and therefore trustworthy workforce". Someone starting in a bank as a junior at 15 years of age could, theoretically at least, progress to the position of general manager or chief cashier with his signature on the bank-notes.

The banking sector started to use mainframe computers in the early sixties where it was used to automate the centralised data systems used by the clearing banks. Nowadays this has progressed to 'data distribution' and 'distributed processing', two differing but related techniques which were devised to overcome one of the major disadvantages of centralised data processing, namely that the data is stored in such a way as to optimise the speed of processing rather than the speed of its retrieval. Thus, today, a bank's data management centre will run two basic types of computer systems; batch systems and on-line systems.

Batch computer systems have existed since the nineteen fifties. This method of running a computer system still has uses in applications such as processing the branch accounts. In such a system a large collection of data already captured, either by physical transportation or via telecommunication links, will be processed at the data processing centre to produce a large collection of output data. The output data, having been produced, is then distributed physically (e.g. account statements posted to the bank's customers) or via telecommunication links (e.g. to the Bank Automated Clearing Service (BACS)).

As the above example illustrates, a batch system may use telecommunication links both to get and distribute its input and output. Since on-line systems also use telecommunication links, what is the key distinction between them? The difference is that the batch system will have all its input data available at the time it begins processing while the on-line system processes the data as it arrives and immediately sends the corresponding output back to the originator of the input. An Automatic Teller Machine (ATM), is a simple example of this.

THE AUTOMATIC TELLER MACHINE (ATM)

The ATM works as follows. When the customer puts his or her card into the machine, the ATM reads the card and account numbers from the magnetic stripe on the card, opens the protective visor and displays a message inviting the customer to enter his or her Personal Identification Number (PIN). The PIN is then encrypted, that is converted into an unreadable code which only the ATM and the central mainframe computer can understand.

The ATM now asks the customer to indicate what service is required. Let us suppose the customer asks to withdraw £100. Until now the ATM has not done anything other than present messages to the customer and encrypt the customer's input. Now it has enough information to pass a request to the central mainframe computer for checking. The ATM constructs a message which says, in effect, "the person who holds the card number xxxxxxxx from account number yyyyyy says that his or her PIN is nnnn and wants to withdraw £100. Should I pay out the money?" It should be noted that the whole message is encrypted so that you would not be able to read it even if you could see it.

Depending on the exact structure of the bank's system, the message will either go to a local mini-computer controlling several ATM's or straight to the bank's data processing centre. There it will be received by a special computer called a teleprocessing front-end computer which is specially configured to handle telecommunications. This computer identifies the type of message being received and directs it to the appropriate mainframe computer. Special software decodes parts of the message and matches it to the right application programme to handle the request.

The application programme compares the encrypted PIN with a copy of the encrypted PIN held on a magnetic disk database. If these and the other details match, and the account details show that the customer has enough funds in his account, then the programme prepares a message which will instruct the ATM to pay the money to the customer. The message passes back to the ATM by the reverse of the original route. When the ATM receives the message it pays out the money to the customer and then sends a second message to the mainframe to say that the customer has received the money. This ensures that when another application programme is run on the mainframe, the customer's records are updated to show that £100 was drawn from an ATM and that amount duly debited from his or her account for that day.

While the procedure seems complex, the entire process takes under 30 seconds and the bank's data processing centre can handle up to thirty separate enquiries of which, perhaps, ten might be from ATM's, every second.

The Clearing System

A British Clearing Bank will use a wide range of computers, typically a small number of mainframes and a larger number of mini-computers, some of which may be connected via telecommunications links to the mainframe computers. They will also make extensive use of private telephone networks, some parts of which will be special very high speed data transfer links such as will BT's 'Kilostream' and 'Megastream'. The Banks also maintain national and international links through the Society for Worldwide Interbank Financial Telecommunications (SWIFT).

As well as using IT to maximise their own efficiencies, the Banks will continue to use IT to provide better and innovative services in order to maintain their client bases in what is now a very competitive marketplace. The Bank of Scotland has been a pioneer in this field with their Home and Office Banking Service, HOBS, introduced early in 1985. Initially HOBS was accessed through the Prestel videotex service but since July 1989 it can be accessed through nodes in the Bank's own private X25 network, and the original HOBS terminals can be replaced by an IBM PC and a modem.

MANUFACTURING

In the diverse realms of manufacturing, IT manifests itself in three main ways:

- reporting and assessing business performance; automation including computer aided design and computer aided management;
- the processing and assimilation of relevant market information.

There is increasing overlap between the first and third of these areas, into what is becoming known variously as Executive Information Systems, EIS, or Management Information Systems, MIS. EIS and MIS will be covered in more detail at the end of this chapter in the section headed 'Information and Management'.

A common problem in the manufacturing sector is that a variety of computer applications have been introduced on an ad hoc basis and are frequently incompatible with each other, as well as failing to meet the needs of other parts of the organisation. An accounting system may work on a different platform from the payroll, warehouse stock control and order-picking might be on another platform while both the computer aided design and management system run on yet another. Introducing a new integrated IT system can represent a very large capital investment and hence it is often put off unless the need to change is catalysed by some external event such as a take-over or relocation.

In many enterprises IT is still viewed with considerable suspicion and senior managements, while they feel sure IT is of benefit, are far from sure how those benefits are derived. It is a situation not unlike that voiced by Lord Leverhulme on the subject of advertising, "Only 50% of my advertising is doing any good, I just don't know which 50%". With the burgeoning power of personal computers coupled with falling prices many companies are tempted to consider downsizing (q.v.).

While many personal computer and network vendors vigorously promote downsizing as a kind of IT panacea, like everything else it has its disadvantages. Apart from the main concerns of the established mainframe user mentioned earlier in this chapter, the greatest of these is the loss of discipline and control inherent in a centralised data processing department. Network users can all too easily customise application programmes themselves without recourse to higher authority, which can result in complete chaos. Elimination of this computer anarchy is probably the greatest challenge facing the manager of a large network of personal computers and the potential for problems in this area has to be fully addressed at the planning stage.

Far-sighted organisations soon realised they would have to integrate the disparate systems in the enterprise to maximise their effectiveness. A growing trend towards vertical integration further reinforced the need to standardise operating platforms in order to meet the increasing demand for detailed information being made at all levels of the organisation. It is this need that has driven the research to create 'open' systems. A fully integrated IT approach could better highlight the performance and profit contribution of non-manufacturing activities such as stock control, warehousing and distribution.

Further upstream in the manufacturing process Computer Aided Design and Computer Aided Manufacture, CAD/CAM, began to be widely adopted in the early eighties. Originally seen as a way to improve the draughtperson's productivity, CAD has progressed far beyond this initial expectation. Nowadays sophisticated CAD systems enable stress and strain analyses to be carried on the screen, and modifications to simplify production engineering can be made rapidly on screen. Instructions for computer controlled machine tools can now be taken from a computer generated drawing and transferred directly to the machine by magnetic tape or disk. Production, from the design engineer's mind to finished component can be done quickly and accurately without recourse to a single sheet of drawing paper. The process is not limited to machined components. The car industry now uses computer controlled automation to make the dies which will shape sheet metal components.

Robots have been introduced widely in some areas of manufacturing, notably welding and printed circuit assembly. Here they have the ability to work faster and more accurately in the manually repetitive tasks where the human performance can deteriorate with the onset of boredom and fatigue. Robots have also been invaluable in replacing humans in hazardous working environments such as the handling of toxic chemicals and radioactive materials.

Finally, whether in CAD or CAM in its widest sense, the adoption of IT in the realms of manufacture is an essential precursor to the adoption of

Total Quality Management, TQM. The implementation of either BS 5750 or ISO 9000 in a manufacturing or service enterprise will be very difficult without an integrated IT system to record and monitor all the data demanded by a modern TQM approach to business.

NEWSPAPERS

Over the past seven years the British newspaper industry has completely meta-morphosed itself from an old-fashioned and inefficient industry crippled by out-dated work practices to a model of high efficiency using state-of-the-art technology based largely on IT. The initial breakthrough was not made in Fleet Street itself but in a number of much smaller provincial newspapers in the early eighties who began to demonstrate the benefits of using the new technologies which had become available.

The history of the ensuing confrontation between the newspaper proprietors and the print unions is well documented elsewhere, although it is questionable if many other industries learned from it. While the proprietors implemented the new technology in different ways, some notably choosing to disperse the printing to smaller units in the provinces, all took the opportunity to, not just implement the new editorial and printing technology but, at the same time, introduce the extensive use of IT to maximise the effect of the extremely expensive investment. The UK national press is a very competitive industry and all the major players have now had to embrace the new technologies just to maintain their position in the marketplace.

For most this has meant the adoption of a four-pronged strategy:

– Use automation to reduce costs of production.

– Introduce flexographic printing technology.

– Speed up the production process right through from copywriting to printed output.

– Introduce computer-based systems to maximise effective management control of the whole business.

A modern newspaper printing plant is now the epitome of high-tech automation controlled by computer. Newsprint, in reels four feet in diameter and weighing nearly two tons are handled automatically all the way from the delivery vehicle to the printing press. Each reel has a barcode which identifies the supplier, mill, grade and so on, and the bar code is read into the plant's computer system which can then follow each and every reel through the plant and any defects in yield and performance reported back to the supplier. The reel store can hold up to 1,000 reels and the control system will know the precise location of every reel, together with all its technical details. The control system reorders newsprint according to pre-programmed instructions regarding rates of consumption and delivery times. Automated reel cranes can move one reel a minute in or out of the store.

An important spin-off of the new technology is that the editorial and management functions need not be located near the presses, traditionally located in the basement in the days of Fleet Street. Newspapers were in fact among the pioneers of teleworking, using various types of telecommunication for a whole range of news gathering activities. Nowadays roving journalists both nationally and internationally can send in their copy using a notebook computer and a modem wherever they are. Journalists based at the head office take advantage of satellite television as well as the myriad of on-line news services and databases to compile their copy. The paper itself is composed using a full blown version of desktop publishing techniques used on personal computers. The completed page layouts are then electronically transmitted to the printing plants either by very large fax machines or as graphical files using a dedicated high capacity data transfer network. This data is fed into platemaking machines which produce the printing plates, now made out of polymer resin.

In parallel with work in the editorial department, the circulation department will be processing sales orders and the results entered into the management computer systems at the printing plant(s) where they are automatically converted into newsprint requirements for the presses as well as all the instructions and timings necessary to meet the constraints of the distribution system. Modern flexographic printing presses run at tremendous speed, two lines of four presses being capable of producing in excess of 500,000 copies per hour. Each press has a 'magazine' holding up to 15 reels of newsprint and as one reel runs out the next new reel is automatically joined to the old one so that paper changes occur without interrupting production.

Printed papers stream on conveyors from the presses to the packing hall where a number of stations count, wrap, strap and label the papers according to the pre-programmed instructions from the circulation department. The labelled bundles then pass over another automatic conveyor system which can read the barcoded labels and thus delivers each bundle to the correct delivery van. Each van driver will already have a note of the number of bundles in his load, together with his planned departure time.

The newspaper industry requires quite exceptional levels of reliability. If delays occur or deadlines missed sales are irretrievably lost. For this reason the newspaper industry has gone to extreme lengths to ensure that its Computer Integrated Management, CIM, systems are as near failsafe as possible and the all key computer hardware is backed up by a standby system already running at 'tick-over'.

In successfully implementing a remarkable programme of change in a fairly short time, the newspaper proprietors are unanimous in their belief that the vital ingredient for the success of the changeover was the time and effort spent on a variety of training and awareness programmes for *all* levels of employees and management. This essential component should always be kept at the forefront of any enterprise's strategy to embark on a programme for the wholesale implementation of IT.

INFORMATION TECHNOLOGY AND MANAGEMENT

In Britain today, management and the personal computer make uneasy bedfellows. Two recent surveys carried out by *'Management Today'* ((11) & (12)) show that just over half (51 percent) of Britain's top executives have a personal computer or a terminal on their desk and that while 76 percent of managers have direct access to screens and keyboards, only 6 percent believe that personal computers are being used to maximum effect in their organisations.

The surveys are a damning indictment of Britain's managerial ability and are a further demonstration that management incompetence is the real reason for the dramatic erosion of the country's manufacturing base. Many British companies are using computers in the worst possible way; to automate manual processes rather than to change work patterns and business practice.

It has been said (13) that information is business's "killer weapon" of the 1990s. A personal computer, either on its own or as part of a network, can with the appropriate software, enable that information to be presented to a manager with only one or two keystrokes. Unfortunately, in Britain many senior managers are oblivious both of how that information might help their businesses or how IT can deliver it.

The owner/manager of the typical small business is all too often 'firefighting' day to day problems or, to put it another way, too busy down in the engine room to come up on to the bridge to see where his ship is going. All too few have the opportunity to sit back and think strategically about their enterprise, or to realise that they could access vital management information if only they knew how.

Virtually every medium and large company will have some level of computerisation, probably with LANs or multiple LANs connected with bridgers or routers. But few companies extend IT to the very top echelons of management where its influence can really matter. There are of course exceptions such as the newspaper industry referred to earlier or the really switched-on companies who pride themselves in delivering their annual results within two weeks of the end of their financial year. Such companies are almost always above-average performers and any bad news they have is announced good and early.

By contrast, one sees with depressing regularity in the financial columns of the newspapers, instances where quite large PLCs suddenly report an unexpected downturn in profits and in some cases move directly into a loss situation. With the present state of IT such lapses are inexcusable and again provide a graphic illustration of how senior management has failed to get to grips with the essential information required to run a commercial enterprise. The technology which can acquire the key information is readily available but there remains an underlying weakness in many senior managements' ability to identify, comprehend and effectively use that information.

An inevitable corollary of this is that apart from the few companies referred to in Chapter 1, few enterprises in Britain have yet considered any of the implications of teleworking. In other countries, notably the USA and Switzerland, teleworking has been widely adopted although has been often directed at overcoming the problem of key skill shortages. Even in recession this still has some relevance in Britain but greater benefits are likely to accrue from cost savings, and improvements in data handling and customer service. In what is becoming an increasingly competitive national and international marketplace, any enterprise ignores these potential advantages at its peril.

It is also true that in many medium to large enterprises who would regard themselves as effective users of IT, senior management has largely shied away from direct contact with the technology, a situation which is borne out by the figures quoted at the beginning of this section. This situation seems set to continue until a new generation of computer literate and IT aware managers inherit the most senior management positions. Unfortunately for some enterprises, this change in attitude at the very top will come too late. The situation is a clear demonstration that in Britain in particular, the constraints to the wider adoption of IT and of course teleworking, are not technological but attitudinal. Changes to such deep-seated and entrenched attitudes are always difficult to implement and will take time to achieve.

Generally it has been financial management, the corporate bean-counters, who have held the growing conviction that IT could help in the better and faster delivery of essential management information. This realisation spawned, in the late seventies, special systems such as Decision Support Systems (DSS) and Management Information Systems (MIS) whose original objectives are fairly self-explanatory. It soon became apparent that DSS and MIS were not going to be the systems that would enable senior executives to manage better, make more informed decisions or otherwise benefit from IT. Something was going to have to be tailor-made for their requirements and that something turned out to be what is now widely known as the Executive Information Systems (EIS).

To begin with there was some inevitable blurring between DSS and EIS but as the concept was refined the differences became quite distinct. It has been suggested (14) that the objectives of an EIS should be to:

– reduce the amount of data bombarding the executive;

– increase the relevance, timeliness and continuing usability of the information that does reach the executive;

– enhance the understanding of the data which is presented;

– facilitate communication with others.

Most EIS are either a user-friendly interface which sits on top of existing database systems such as accounting or stock control packages, or a stand-alone system which will incorporate information from outside as well as inside the enterprise. The importance of the latter type of system can be readily appreciated in today's frantic business climate where bank and exchange rates change on almost a daily basis. As well as these two vital factors, stand-alone systems can also readily incorporate up-to-the minute market data as well as information about the competition.

An EIS usually works by monitoring a number of critical factors identified by the executives running the business. They are called either Key Performance Indicators (KPI) or Critical Success Factors (CSF). Performance targets are then set and the system is then programmed to measure the chosen factors against the targets and to highlight any variation of these factors outside present limits. As well as these essential requirements, most EIS will have additional capabilities such as exception reporting, trend analysis and a 'drill down' facility.

'Drill down' is a facility which enables the user to progressively examine the information presented on screen in increasing detail. For example, the sales for one month can be seen on successive screens by country, by region, by product or by distributor. Or the payroll for a month can be seen as a global total which can then be progressively examined by location, department and even job grade and that information matched to performance.

At the present time EIS do not come cheap and they tend to be custom designed to meet the client's specific needs. Costs vary from £15,000 for a modest installation to in excess of £250,000 for a fully fledged system in a large organisation. Consequently, installation decisions have to be made at the highest level and it is often difficult to quantify the benefits of an EIS to a sceptical board of directors. While a number of accounting application programmes based on a database format now have a limited reporting function, e.g. credit control, as yet there is only one stand-alone EIS package available off the shelf as it were, 'Forest & Trees' (European Software Publishing) which is 'Windows'-based and designed to be configured by the user.

CONCLUSION

There is probably no-one in a developed country such as Britain whose life today is not affected in some way by a facet of IT. Considerable computing power is available to all for a relatively low cost, together with equally inexpensive applications software. Yet in the workplace or even in the home, all too few enterprises or individuals are maximising their use of the available technology. To the prospective teleworker, a widening appreciation and adoption of IT represents greater and more innovative work opportunities. While some business sectors are clearly further ahead than others, Britain at least has a long way to go before it can be said to be taking full advantage of IT.

Some have likened Information Technology to the second industrial revolution. It would be a tragedy if Britain in particular, the country that was the birthplace of the first industrial revolution allowed itself to be overtaken by the second, especially if that failure was a result of indifference and resistance to change.

3 Telecommunication Links

BACKGROUND

Until 1981 the sole responsibility for the telephone network in the UK (with the exception of the city of Hull) lay with the government owned General Post Office (GPO). With a few minor exceptions such as large company switchboards, all business and domestic customers had to rent telephones lines, telephones, telexes and so on from the GPO. This meant a poor service with a limited choice of equipment which was manufactured to GPO specifications by a number of third party suppliers. The overall result was that by the end of the seventies, Britain had an expensive and obsolescent telephone network.

All this was to change with the introduction, in the summer of 1981, of the Telecommunications Act (1981). This was to radically change the provision of telecommunications within the UK. The Act contained four main features:

1. The creation of British Telecom from what was Post Office Telecommunications, the Post Office retaining the mail services.

2. The introduction of competition in the supply of telecommunication equipment to business and domestic customers, subject to its approval, by the British Approvals Board for Telecommunications (BABT).

3. The introduction of competition in the supply of telecommunication lines and Mercury Telecommunication Ltd given a 25 year licence to compete with British Telecom.

4. The introduction of value added network services, such as electronic mailboxes and voice messaging, through third party suppliers.

The Office of Telecommunications (OFTEL) was established in 1984 to act as the industry's watchdog and to ensure that full and fair competition existed between the companies in the new industry.

TELEX

Telex is the British Telecom teleprinter service for business users. The 'Vidiprinter' used for football results is a version of a telex machine.

A telex message is usually prepared prior to transmission although experienced operators can use them 'live' or 'on-line'. Early telex terminals used punched paper tape as the storage medium but this has now been superceded by electronic memory. Once the message has been prepared, the number of the receiving terminal is dialled in the conventional way and when contact has been made both terminals exchange what are known as 'answerback codes'. This exchange of codes ensures that the correct terminal has been contacted, and that the sending terminal is in transmit mode while the receiving terminal is in receive mode. The message is then transmitted and simultaneously received. The rate of telex transmission is fairly slow, about seventy words per minute.

The telex's great advantage was that it produced hard copy and countless commercial deals have been concluded on the basis of a telexed order. The log-on log-off procedure of the telex gives better security than a fax machine, which can be configured to appear as though it is somewhere else. The service has good global coverage with over 2 million users worldwide and over 100,000 in the UK. The main disadvantages of the telex are its low speed and that it uses dedicated telegraph lines for transmission which are more expensive to rent than phone lines while using a more primitive technology.

While new sophisticated electronic telex terminals have been developed, the telex system can be said to have reached its zenith. The arrival of the facsimile (fax) machine heralded the beginning of the end for the telex. In addition, the telephone companies (PTTs) are focussing the investment into digital and optical networks, while there is a growing trend away from the dedicated telex terminal to personal computer based systems.

THE FAX MACHINE

The fax machine has to be regarded as one of the commercial wonders of recent years. From a high-tech curio in a few avant garde offices it has developed at an extraordinary rate to become the most essential business machine after the telephone. Prices have fallen to the level where a simple fax costs less than a washing machine. The catchphrase now is "don't post it, fax it". It can transmit and receive virtually anything that can be put on a piece of paper, quickly and cheaply and of course it uses the existing telephone networks.

The concept of the fax machine was first enunciated in 1842 by a Scottish philosopher, Alexander Bain (1818–1903). Bain showed how any document could be encoded, the code transmitted and an exact copy of the document reconstructed from the code. Exploitation of the concept was slow due to obvious limitations in the available technology of the day and it was first used to send photographs by cable. Early progress of the fax machine as we know it today was dogged by differing transmission standards being adopted by the manufacturers. This was eventually resolved by the Comité Consultatif International de Téléphonie et de Télégraphie, CCITT, who produced standards for four groups of machines. Group 3 is now regarded as the industry norm while Group 4 machines are for use on high speed ISDN lines.

A fax machine works by dividing the paper to be scanned into a large number of discrete dots. In transmitting mode, a photo-electric detector measures the amount of light from a fluorescent lamp reflected back from each dot and sends the resulting pulses down the telephone line to the receiving machine. In receiving mode, the incoming pulses go to a thermal print head which converts them to visible dots on heat-sensitive paper. Fax machines 'talk' to each other to establish the communicating protocol and which mode is required by a series of squeaks and chirrups which we have all heard when we have inadvertently dialled a fax machine.

The fax's huge success is due primarily to its relative cheapness both in capital and running costs, its flexibility in that it can send all sorts of images and is not restricted to typewritten or printed text and, finally its ease of operation. Fax users should heed one word of caution. Thermal-imaging on to heat sensitive paper is not notably stable and any fax that is to be put in an archive should first be transferred to a more stable photocopy. Plain paper fax machines, which do not have this problem, are available but are very expensive.

DIGITAL TELEPHONE SYSTEMS

The continuous developments of the telephone networks has, from their inception, been driven by two fundamental requirements. The first has been the need to cater for ever increasing volumes of telephonic traffic and the second has been to meet that demand without loss in quality due to noise or interference.

The telephone's invention came out of attempts to develop a 'multiplex' telegraph system. Multiplexing is the term for sending a number of different messages along the same wire at the same time. The creation of the telephone simply moved the goal posts and subsequent research went into devising multiplexing techniques for the telephone.

The microphone in a telephone handset produces an anal*ogue* electrical signal, that is to say it has a waveform which varies in an *analogous* way to the sound waves that formed them. Several techniques were developed so that a number of separate messages could be carried over the same telephone line. However, the analogue technology was limited and a hundred-odd years after its introduction, telephony moved into the digital era.

In a digital system the sound from the microphone is rapidly sampled (8,000 times a second) and each sample value is expressed in binary form, each value being represented by a series of ones or zeros. This technique is known as **encoding**. At the receiving end the binary signal is decoded back into analogue form and thence to the earpiece. Without going into a highly technical dissertation, suffice it to say that digital technology allows far higher levels of traffic with much less interference than the analogue system.

Another development which has further increased the advantages of digital telephony has been the introduction of the fibre optic cable. These can carry very many more messages than copper cable, and are immune to any electrical interference from inside or outside the cable. Fibre optic cables consist of a large number of very fine glass strands packed together inside a tough protective casing. The messages are carried down the individual fibres by means of a stream of laser light pulses which travel down the strand of fibre at the speed of light. A laser beam is a beam of light with a very specific wavelength or colour, in fact ruby red. The computerised telephone exchange converts the electrical signal of a telephone call into laser light pulses. When the pulses reach the exchange at the far end they are converted back to electricity and are sent down a conventional copper wire to the telephone called.

At this time, all of the Mercury network and most of British Telecom's long distance cables are fibre optic. All Mercury's exchanges are digital while around 35 percent of BT's have been converted, mostly in country areas. BT's customer service will be able to tell you if you are on a digital exchange.

Medium and heavy users of the telephone such as teleworkers should always remember that in an increasingly large number of places the Mercury network can offer significant reductions in call charges. Many BT subscribers can reach the Mercury network through local access points, and then benefit from Mercury's cheaper long distance charges. For further information one should contact the local Mercury office or call 0800 424 194.

We are told that to meet ever increasing demand BT will be revising all our telephone numbers within the next five years, repeating no doubt the fun and games when the London area changed to two codes a few years ago. The writer would like to ask BT to use this opportunity to introduce some semblance of logic into our current telephone exchange code system. At present, British telephone numbers have between eight and ten digits. Two exchanges with codes in sequence can be hundreds of miles apart while, for other than the major cities, glancing at a code gives no clue as to its location. Surely we can follow North America where numbers all have an area code, usually placed in parenthesis, followed by a three digit exchange followed by a four digit number.

As well as BT and Mercury public switched telephoned networks there are a number of special networks called Packet Switch Stream, PSS, which have high speed data transmission capabilities. The commonest one in the UK is Istel and a teleworker can dial the nearest Istel number or 'node' through a modem and be connected into the system and thence to a database service such as Prestel or Compuserve.

MICROWAVES AND SATELLITES

Microwaves are electromagnetic radiation of very high frequency, from 1 GigaHertz (one thousand million cycles per second) to 1 TeraHertz (one million million cycles per second). They therefore have corresponding short wavelengths, between 1 millimetre and 1 metre. Apart from their well-known heating properties in the microwave oven, they are widely used for data transmission.

Microwave transmission has a very high speed capability of over 100,000 characters per second. Their disadvantages are that they travel only in straight lines and they have a limited range of about 25 to 30 miles through the dense atmosphere close to the earth's surface. Therefore microwave links have to have a number of repeater stations, each one in line of sight from the other. The signals are sent and received from parabolic reflector dishes such as those which can be seen on the Post Office Tower in London. In spite of these limitations microwave links can be very cost effective over difficult terrain.

Microwaves are also used as the telecommunication link to satellites. The idea of a communication satellite was first proposed by the British scientific author Arthur C. Clarke in 1945. The first successful telecommunication satellite was 'Telstar' which was launched in July 1962. The first synchronous communication satellite was 'Syncom 2' launched in July 1963.

Synchronous communication satellites orbit the earth at a height of about 23,000 miles, at which distance the speed required to maintain that orbit results in an orbiting time which is the same as the earth's. The satellite thus appears to an observer on earth to stay in the same place and such satellites are said to be in a 'geo-stationary' orbit. The microwaves' range is largely unaffected going straight up through the atmosphere although the incoming signals are sufficiently weak to require a large satellite dish aerial to receive them.

International non-military satellite communications are controlled by the organisation Intelsat. It was formed in 1964 by 11 countries and launched its first satellite, Intelstat 1, in 1965.   Intelstat 1 could handle 240 two-way telephone conversations or one television channel. By contrast, current satellites can handle around 60 television channels or 30,000 telephone circuits. The Intelstat system has now expanded into over 150 countries and there are about 600 earth stations.

MODEMS

The modem (modulator—demodulator) is teleworking's raison d'etre. It is the little black box through which a computer can talk to another computer using a telephone line. Unfortunately for the teleworker, no computer peripheral is so shrouded in mystery or arouses such a love/hate response as the modem. This section endeavours to cut away at least some of the mystique and explain the basic principles in plain language. The modem is, after all, the keystone of the teleworking concept.

The modem was devised to convert the electrical signals that routinely move backwards and forwards inside a computer into a form that could be sent along the public switched telephone network, PSTN. The PSTN was designed to handle voice messages and consequently does not have the capacity to send very many signals per second. This capacity is measured in units called baud or signals per second, and the PSTN has a usable capacity of about 2,400 baud. As modems need to send data in both directions at the same time, this means that the theoretical maximum speed of communication is 1,200 bits per second, bps.

This speed was far too slow given the vast amounts of data required for inter-computer conversation, so modem manufacturers have progressively devised more and more advanced modulation techniques in order to stuff even more data down a telephone line each second. For this reason there is a difference between the baud rate and the transfer rate, bps. The baud rate refers to the capacity of the phone line, bps to the speed of the data passing along the line. As in the early stages of fax machine development, the early days of computer communications were hampered by differing standards; these differences have now been resolved and all international standards are approved by the CCITT and these standards are prefixed by the letter V.

The earliest standard was V21, 300bps followed by V22, 1,200bps and then V22bis, 2,400bps. V32, 9,600bps was agreed in 1984 although it took the modem manufacturers several years before they could produce modems to meet this new standard. The latest standard is V32bis, 14,400bps. A future standard, already referred as V. Fast is being negotiated at the present time by the CCITT and will probably support 24,000bps. To confuse the issue, some sets of V numbers do not refer to speed standards. V25bis is a standard which enables a personal computer to talk to a mainframe or mini computer while V42 and V42bis refer to methods of error correction.

This pursuit of speed has not just been about reducing the phone charges incurred when using a modem. Computer files, particularly program files, are getting larger all the time. One notable story relates to an American programmer who dutifully dialled up his head office through his modem and started to upload his new program. He then put some floppy disks containing the program into his pocket and cycled the ten miles to the head office. He arrived before the program had finished being uploaded. Not too many teleworkers will be moving such large amounts of data around but the story illustrates the reason behind the inexorable drive towards faster and faster rates of data transfer.

There are two magic words any prospective modem purchaser has to look for; 'Hayes Compatible'. Dennis Hayes, the founder of the American company Hayes Microcomputer Products is sometimes referred to as the father of the modem. Hayes devised a new way of controlling a modem from a personal computer called the 'AT command set' and this has now been adopted by every modem maker of note. As well as a modem being 'Hayes Compatible' it goes without saying that it must have the BABT green blob of approval.

The speed and reliability with which data can be transferred over ordinary telephone lines is due in no small part to the development of new techniques for error correction and data compression. Apart from the aforementioned V42 and V42bis, the most widely accepted standards for error correction have been set by Miracom Technology with their Miracom Network Protocols, MNP. MNP 5 is the most widely used while the newer MNP 10 is 'state-of-the-art' technology. While error correction slows down the throughput of data, the loss of speed is compensated by the use of data compression techniques.

An interesting new development of special interest to teleworkers is the fax modem. This is a modem which has a fax card grafted on to it. With a fax modem a letter can be sent from a word processing program directly to a dedicated Group 3 fax machine without creating a piece of paper. The disadvantages of a fax card or a fax modem are that one's personal computer has to be left on at all times to receive incoming material and that one cannot, of course, sign the document.

Modems come in a variety of sizes and can be fitted inside notebook computers as well as desktop models. Prices range from £300 to £1,000 for a top range unit. Leading brands are Hayes, Miracom, Dowty, Pace and Racal. Virtually all modems will come packaged with communication software which is covered in detail in the next section.

COMMUNICATIONS SOFTWARE

Like all personal computer peripherals, a modem cannot work without the appropriate software. 'Comms' software comes in two main varieties. Plain comms programs simply drive the modem and let you move data to and collect data from a remote computer. The fancier 'remote control' packages enable one to take full control of the remote computer as if your keyboard had become its keyboard. We'll consider basic comms programs first.

The two essentials of a comms programme are its dialling directory and its file transfer protocols. As one might expect, a dialling directory is a list of the telephone numbers that are used regularly, together with all the details of the settings used to connect to the modem and computer on that number. These settings will consist of the speed, in bps, data, usually 7 or 8, parity, N for no or E for even and stop bits, usually 1. These settings have to be identical to those of the computer and modem with which you are communicating. It is also vital to know which serial port your modem is connected to, usually COM1 or COM2.

When a modem is instructed to dial a number you will first hear a dialling tone (all modems have a small loudspeaker) and then the sound of the modem dialling the number, followed by the ringing tone, assuming the line is not engaged, just as though you were using an ordinary phone. When the call is answered by another modem you will hear some weird whistles and squeaks as the two modem try to establish a connection with each other and decide what speed to operate at and which protocols to use. This process is know as 'handshaking'. After a few seconds things should go quiet and your computer monitor will show that you are connected to another computer or database service.

A modem can, and as far as a teleworker is concerned, should be set up to accept incoming calls, a state that is known as being in 'host' mode. A good comms program will let you set up your modem in such a way that it can be readily switched or "toggled" as they say in computer parlance, between call mode, its usual state and auto answer mode, a state that is normally disabled.

It has to be said that configuring a comms program and getting a modem to work satisfactorily can try the patience of a saint. This situation is not helped by instruction manuals often written in excruciating English and full of obscure technical jargon. Perseverance usually pays off in the end and results in a warm feeling of real achievement. However, if all else fails get some help from a local computer specialist; you should be able to track one down using the Yellow Pages.

Once one has contacted or 'logged on' to the other computer the teleworker will want to transfer files. Receiving files from another computer is called downloading, sending files to the other machine is called uploading. Files are transferred using what are called transfer protocols and the three most common ones rejoice in the imaginative names of Xmodem, Ymodem and Zmodem. Xmodem is widely used but slow, Ymodem is faster but does not have any error correction ability. Zmodem is the best. It is fast and allows one to resume a file transfer that has been interrupted. Zmodem can also be used with one of the error correction protocols such as MNP 5 or V42.

As well as transferring files backwards and forwards, these basic comms programs enable one to access Bulletin Board Services, BBS, and database services. BBSs can be electronic mail services, helpline services or a special interest chatlines. The two largest BBSs are Compuserve and CIX, both based in the USA but accessed in the UK by local Istel numbers. More details of the numerous BBSs can be found in the specialist computer magazines. A useful general database is the Prestel service while the 'Manchester Host' service is a gateway to more than 120 specialised databases covering such diverse topics as health and safety, finance and business, news and travel, sociology and science and technology. The Manchester Host scheme has a registration charge and then charges so much per minute, depending on the database being used. Remember that you will have telephone charges in addition to the access fees.

Security, or rather the lack of it, is often seen as a weakness of computer communication systems. All comms software has some form of password protection but the most powerful and elegant protection is what is known as 'callback'. With 'callback', when anyone logs into a computer, the host modem immediately hangs up and then redials the remote computer on a pre-programmed number before allowing any access to data. Thus while a speculative 'hacker' could access a company computer by chance, he won't be doing it from a number recognised by the computer and the attempt will be foiled.

Remote control software takes the use of the modem even further; you do not simply transfer files, you take full control of the remote computer from your own keyboard. Remote control software is still in its infancy and at present is seriously hobbled by the speeds of even the fastest modems and the limitations of the various disk operating systems for personal computers, notably MS-DOS for the PC. Remote control cannot be seriously recommended at speeds below 9,600bps; one does not want to wait ten seconds or more to see your instructions transferred to the screen. Most remote control programs get round this by transferring the screen image intermittently. When DOS was created, the idea of graphic screens and the concept of remote control were not even smudges on the horizon. Consequently, remote control software has to use subterfuge to trick DOS into doing things it would rather not do and these are not always successful. Some perfectly compliant DOS application programs will steadfastly refuse to work by remote control.

At this time one has to say that remote control programs are in the 'not for novices' category. However, teleworking 'power users' should certainly find something to meet their needs and which will respond to a fair degree of fine tuning and tweaking. 'Reachout' and 'pcAnywhere' are two such programs which have received considerable critical acclaim.

ISDN

Integrated Services Digital Network, ISDN is a fully digital telecommunications network designed to allow the transmission of high volumes of electronic data as well as high quality voice messaging via a single digital connection to a new digital public network system. As has been stated earlier, above, both BT and Mercury are already using digital technology on their main trunk routes for conventional calls. ISDN extends the digital facility right into the office and the home.

While ISDN has not been conspicuously successful in the USA, it is being vigorously implemented in Europe. It will be available in all twelve member states of the EEC by the end of 1993, as well as Japan, Australia, Hong Kong and Singapore in the Far East. In Britain about 60 per cent of subscribers are already connected to digital exchanges which can offer the ISDN service. BT say that on average two more exchanges are being converted every week, and the entire network should be digital by 1996/7.

In the UK, BT offers ISDN at two different levels. ISDN 30 is designed principally for large organisations and has 30 channels for voice and data as well as signalling and synchronisation channels. It is BT's other system ISDN 2 which is of particular interest to the teleworker.

ISDN 2 has two channels for voice and data and one for signalling. The system transfers information at a rate of 144,000bps, which is then split into two user channels of 64,000bps and a signal channel of 16,000bps. The two user channels can be used simultaneously and for different purposes; eg data and voice. The system can also access the normal telephone network in the usual way. BT provide a small wall mounted unit which is used to connect terminal equipment to the ISDN. Up to eight items of terminal equipment can be connected to an ISDN 2 line using BT approved wiring. ISDN 2 can be configured in a number of different ways. There can be one exchange number per line or one number per channel or one number for each item of terminal equipment such as a fax machine, a personal computer or a telephone.

Using ISDN removes the need for a modem. An adapter card which fits into one of the computer's expansion slots is used instead. This card connects with the ISDN terminal using an RJ45 plug. ISDN adapter cards for personal computers are made by IBM, Gravatom Technology and Maxim Networks.

The charges for ISDN are not unreasonable given their enormous capacity for data reception and transmission. The ISDN 2 connection charge is £470.00 and quarterly rental is £98.70, both inclusive of VAT. There are fairly modest additional charges for the multiple subscriber numbering facility. Call charges are the same as for the ordinary BT network.

ISDN is the future in telecommunications. As well as very high speed data transmission, new horizons are opening such as video-conferencing,

Videotex access to databases and high quality audio capabilities. The sky is, very nearly, the limit.

BT clearly has high hopes for ISDN, which has the potential to be the UK's *de facto* telephone network by the year 2010. So far their marketing efforts for ISDN leave something to be desired. Seminars promoting ISDN tend to be full of IT professionals preaching to the converted while not enough is yet being done to explain to ordinary businessmen how ISDN can help their companies and improve the bottom line.

4 Telecottages and Satellite Offices

The concept of the Community Telecommunication Centre (CTC), Electronic Village Hall (EVH), or Telecottage as it is more commonly known, was started in Scandinavia in the mid-eighties. The idea was pioneered by Henning Albrechtsen, a linguist and one-time chief interpreter to the United Nations. Albrechtsen had retired to a remote village, Vemdalen, some 250km north west of Gävle in northern Sweden, and was concerned about the lack of job opportunities for young people in his and other such villages. Although he had only just become familiar with the personal computer, Albrechtsen had the foresight to see the potential of the personal computer, used in conjunction with the new advances in telecommunications, to access remote information services and so negate some of these areas' geographical disadvantages.

He set up in Vemdalen, what is widely regarded as the world's first telecottage, which in time became a veritable mecca visited by many special interest groups from all over the world. It was from Albrechtsen's Vemdalen venture that the whole telecottage idea took off. In Britain the first telecottage was set up in 1989 and the concept has now gained considerable momentum with over forty established nationwide, mainly in the north of England, Wales and the Highlands and Islands of Scotland.

The use of the word 'telecottage' is already a contentious issue. It has already been forcefully stated that to be successful the services provided by teleworking have to be completely transparent and totally professional and many workers in the field feel that the name 'telecottage' instantly negates that impression. The concept has already attracted considerable press coverage and reports of telecottages located in converted barns staffed by part-timers who have just finished tending their goats does not always convey the right impression to potential clients in big business. While there is no doubt someone will devise a more appropriate name for them, the word telecottage is used throughout this book.

In its original form, a telecottage is a computer-based information centre in a country village and provides the local community with access to information technology they could not otherwise afford and to data normally held in large centres of population. Although they were initially seen as a way of reversing rural depopulation and to help regenerate the local economies, it was quickly seen that they would have to progress beyond that primary remit of data transmission and retrieval if they were to be viable.

Telecottages cost money; for equipment, premises and personnnel and their cosss could not be sustained if they operated only as a electronic reference library. Thus telecottages have had to adopt a multi-faceted approach in order to achieve self-sufficiency through the services they offered and are now seen as IT training centres, computer bureaux, electronic sorting offices and electronic noticeboards as well as support centres for local teleworkers. Perhaps the most important contribution of the telecottage to the growth of teleworking in general will be as rural focal points of teleworking from which knowledge and training will spread outwards into the rest of the community.

The major impediment to the spread of telecottages in Britain has been money, especially the initial seed capital for hardware, software and premises as well as the running costs. Hardware costs are presently decreasing almost daily and with some innovative thought, rent-free premises or even a single room can be found in most villages. A trainer/manager on the other hand is going to cost around £15,000 per annum and with heat, light, power, insurances and so forth, a telecottage's annual running costs will be around £25,000. To ensure a telecottage's long-term survival, these costs have ultimately to be recovered from the services provided.

In Britain, the main sources of funding are likely to be the Training and Enterprise Councils, TECs in England and Wales and the Local Enterprise Companies, LECs in Scotland. Local councils can also be helpful and those areas of the country which have EEC funded development schemes are particularly fortunate as the EEC looks very favourably on all aspects of teleworklng. Any proposals for funding from any authority have to be supported by a well thought out and presented business plan just like any other business venture. All local authorities are currently operating under severe financial constraint, and the days when large amounts of public largesse were sloshing round the system looking for a good home have long gone. A section dealing with the compilation of an effective business plan is to be found at the beginning of Chapter 10.

British Telecom itself has been prominent in providing funding, notably in the Highlands and Islands and, through its Community Action programme, has helped to fund four variants of the telecottage, the TeleService Centre. BT also provide some of the funding to 'Action with Communities in Rural England', ACRE, which is very much the catalyst and umbrella organisation for the telecottage movement in the United Kingdom. ACRE (15) is a registered charity and as well as running seminars, conferences and workshops on telecottages and teleworking produces a newsletter and number of factsheets. A contact number for ACRE can be found in Appendix 2.

Among the hardware manufacturers, only the Apple Corporation have appreciated the potential of this market and offer a selection of their computers to bona fide telecottages for very nominal rents. Details of the Apple scheme can be obtained through ACRE.

Confirming the need for a multi-faceted approach, ACRE has produced a concise list of services that could be offered by a telecottage although these will depend on the level of local expertise that is available:

–   Audio Typing

–   Book-keeping/Accountancy Services

–   Computer Programming/Software Support

–   Data Input

–   Desktop Publishing

–   Employment Brokerage

–   Equipment rental

_   Faxing/Copying/Laser Printing

–   Local Facilities Booking Agency

–   Local Information Service

–   Message Taking Service

- Mailing List Compilation
- Market Research
- Mail Shot Service
- On-line Database Research
- Proof reading
- Technical Writing
- Telephone Sales
- Training Services
- Translation Services
- Word Processing/Report Writing

An in-depth treatment of the marketing and selling of teleworked services including those which can be provided by a telecottage is given in Chapter 7.

In Britain there has been considerable diversity in telecottage objectives and not all have been successful. While the majority regard IT as their raison d'etre, in some it is just one component in a range of services that they provide. There is also variety in the target users of the facility. Some direct their services to the small businesses and their local community at large, while others may focus on a specific group such as women, a particular ethnic or religious culture, or the disabled. The following section will give some indication of the wide range of activities and problems that have been encountered by some telecottages in the UK.

BRITISH TELECOTTAGES

The Moorlands Telecottage in the village of Warslow at the southern end of the Peak District was Britain's first telecottage and opened in late 1989. It is located in the local primary school. The telecottage is run as a partnership between Staffordshire County Council Youth and Community Programme, Leek College and Staffordshire Training and Enterprise Council. There is also some additional funding through the EEC Euroform Programme.

The Moorlands Telecottage was seen by its sponsors as being a vital component of the Warslow Community Education Project. Its comprehensive prospectus (16), is a model of its kind, and demonstrates the breadth of the multi-faceted approach and for that reason is worth quoting verbatim:

"Community Development   This will involve supporting the activities of local community groups such as Playgroups and Parish Councils etc., by allowing them access to Information Technology resources. Specific areas of support are likely to be:

—   to allow access to Wordprocessing, Database and Accounting facilities so that groups may operate more effectively.

—   to allow access to Desktop Publishing Facilities so groups may improve the spread of information about their activities, enabling them to reach a wider audience.

—   to provide access to on-line database facilities and other information sources as a way of improving the access to information services available in the Moorlands area.

—   by acting as a focal point for certain activities, the Telecottage has a role to play in strengthening community identity and encouraging a greater degree of interdependence between the Moorland communities.

"Education and Training This will involve the use of the Telecottage to provide access to a variety of training and educational opportunities on a local basis. Specific areas of provision are likely to be:

—   to provide extra information technology resources to the local school that can be used to enhance areas of the lschool curriculum.

—   to allow members of the local community access to information technology equipment so that they may acquire familiarity and skills in its use.

—   to provide local training opportunities so that individuals may gain skills in information technology, etc.

—   to provide local training opportunities and familiarisation in the use of information technology for small businesses such as farms and rural workshops. Such activities are likely to involve collaboration with other training agencies.

Local Economic Development The Telecottage will be used to provide a range of services and opportunities that will be aimed at developing the local economy. Specific activities will include:

- to provide a range of office-style services such as Wordprocessing, Document typing, Invoicing, Telephone answering, Desktop Publishing and Facsimile services, etc., to support small rural businesses.

- to provide flexible local employment opportunities in the provision of the above services.

- to provide access to informatiom technology equipment so that local people may learn to use them and thus gain employment by teleworking.

- to import high quality employment opportunities of a teleworking nature into the area and to make these available to local people.

The Moorlands Telecottage and Community Education The Telecottage will address all of the six core areas of Community Education. For example:

- Adult Education – it will provide a range of Adult Education opprtunities which are presently not available locally and for which there is a demand.

- Community Access to Local Education Authority – it will be an L.E.A. resource which will be used by the local community.

- Advice and Information – by providing access to on-line databases the Telecottage will greatly enhance the availability of advice and information locally.

- *Youth Provision* – by using telecommunication links it will be possible for local youth clubs to engage in interaction with other youth clubs as a process of social education.

- Curriculum Enhancement – telecottage computers will provide additional resources for valuable hands-on experience for chool pupils.

- Community Development – supporting the work of community groups and stimulating the local economy will have a significant influence on improving the quality of life in the Moorlands area."

In addition to the core activities, as set out in the above prospectus, the Moorlands Telecottage is a partner in a pan-European project which is trying to develop a new "transnational" vocational qualification for Teleworkers. The project, which is part funded by the EEC under the EUROFORM grant scheme, has partners in Devon, Ireland, Portugal, Spain and Italy. A training programme will cover the three broad topic areas which represent the range of skills an individual needs to operate as a teleworker. These skill areas are:

- The use of computers and application programmes.

- Business Administration.

- Business and Self Development Skills.

It is anticipated that this training will lead to a New Vocational Qualification in Teleworking and it is intended that the qualification will be validated by City and Guilds.

It has taken three years for the Moorlands Telecottage to more or less attain financial self sufficiency. Apart from some subsidies from the Education Project its income now covers its costs and it is beginning to consider plans to upgrade and buy new equipment. While the telecottage has not directly created many jobs its newly qualified trainees have found it much easier to find employment in the area. The Moorlands management feel that the impact of the telecottage would have been greater had it employed a full-time manager from day one, a position which the limited start up funds did not permit. They also felt that the enthusiasm and personality of the telecottage manager or supervisor play a crucial role in ensuring success.

The **Antur Tanat Cain Telebureau** in Wales, some eight miles south-west of Oswestry started in a rather different way. A derelict mill at Llangedwyn was restored in 1986 by the local County Council to provide a number of small business or craft workshops for a peppercorn rent. One unit was rented as a base for a survey of local headstones in churchyards, the information being stored on a personal computer database.

From this modest beginning ATCT has progressed to being a qualified IT training provider and is now in a position to tender for data processing contracts for business and government departments having achieved full telebureau status. The Telebureau is run as a community charity and all the proceeds are ploughed back in to progressively expand the Telebureau's facilities. It has trained over 200 people, many of them women returning to the workplace, while more than 50 had gone on to acquire the Royal Society of Arts Diploma in IT.

The Telebureau has been particularly successful in obtaining data processing contracts from third parties and according to the Telebureau's manager, Paddy Moindrot, the key to this has been the demonstrable imposition of quality control checks and supervision. The Telebureau initially hired the services of an outside consultant to draw up control procedures and this was instumental in helping the Telebureau secure its first contract. Others have subsequently followed and the Telebureau has extended its services into the realms of Welsh language translation and desktop publishing.

The **Warwick Rural Enterprise Network**, or **WREN** telecottage is located on the Royal Agricultural Society's showground at Stoneleigh in Warwickshire. Opened at the beginning of 1992, WREN is aimed very much at women returning to the workplace and to this end it provides a nursery facility with three full-time staff which can accommodate up to twelve children. As well as IT training it offers computer bureau services and business advice and support to enterprises in the locality.

The main thrust of WREN's philosophy in its dealings with the local business community has been to emphasise collaboration rather competition. Affirming this approach WREN has a mobile training trailer which it uses to take its training courses to the business customer. In assessing this innovative scheme, one must remember that WREN is different from most other telecottages. While located in a rural setting, it is in the centre of a very densely populated area. WREN currently employs two full-time and two part-time staff and is equipped with both Apple Mac and IBM PC computers.

As part of their ambitious strategy to become Europe's foremost IT oriented city, Manchester City Council have initiated an innovative variant of the telecottage in an urban environment, the Electronic Village Hall (EVH). Six EVH's have been set up and another ten are being planned. As always, finding funds has been difficult with three of the EVH's obtaining working capital from a 'City Action Team' and British Telecom initiative.

The **Chorlton Workshop EVH** is unusual in that the workshop was an established but struggling community centre when it applied to become an EVH. The Chorlton project has concentrated on training for the unemployed with no computer experience as well as courses for the more advanced student. To generate income Chorlton offers courses in well known WP and DTP programmes. It is proposed in future to offer courses leading to the RSA Certificate and Diploma in IT.

The **Bangladesh House EVH** was opened in March 1992 and as its name suggests is directed at bringing IT to the extensive Bangladeshi community in the city. As well as training leading to RSA qualifications, the BHEVH naturally concentrates on providing business and DTP services for the whole Asian community and has found that its expertise in non-roman scripts has attracted interest from the former Eastern Bloc countries.

The Women's EVH is based at the Gita Bhavan Community Centre and while it is the first EVH specifically designed to meet the varied needs of women, it also has an ethnic bias. While many women already have keyboard skills and some degree of computer literacy, most are in low paid and low status jobs. The main thrust of the Women's EVH is to help and encourage women to use IT to improve their job prospects as well as for social purposes. Among the key features of the Women's EVH are courses run throughout the day and evening to accommodate the women's other obligations, a free creche facility, and, most important for some religions, an all female staff of managers and trainers.

The main thrust of the **Rosset Telecottage** near Wrexham is to promote IT and teleworking to people with learning difficulties. The telecottage is supported by a local Work Opportunities initiative and provides training and work experience to disadvantaged young people whilst maintaining commercial viability. So far two of its protégés have passed their first RSA exams, with no concessions being made for their disabilities. As well as offering the usual range of business services, Rosset has negotiated with a mail order catalogue company to start a teleshopping service from the telecottage thus increasing local community involvement.

Scotland is in an especially strong position to take full advantage of teleworking since it is the first large area of the United Kingdom to have a completely digital telephone network. The provision of this infrastructure enabled Teleworking to be considered as one solution to help reverse the trend of rural depopulation. In the Spring of 1991 Highlands and Islands Enterprise and British Telecom jointly provided funding to set up and operate for an initial two year period, six experimental Community Teleservice Centres, five on islands and one on the mainland, in Argyll.

The **Isles Telecroft** is situated at the northern extremity of the British Isles, on the Shetland island of Unst. The Telecroft was opened in May 1991 and is a subsidiary of North Isles Community Enterprises. It employs a project manager, an office manager and a training manager who are all qualified trainers with Scottish Vocational Education Council (SCOTVEC) qualifications. Its main objective is to be a working example of some of the applications of IT to the people of the North Isles (of Shetland) and to provide opportunities for social and economic development.

The Telecroft has managed a project for the local museum in Lerwick for which it recruited four trainees from nearby islands. By the conclusion of the project, creating a database of the museum's artefacts, the trainees will have acquired the RSA qualification in IT and will be in a position to take that knowledge back to their own islands. The Telecroft's next project, called "New Abilities" will be aimed at training disabled people in computer skills and giving them some work experience in the new technology.

Argyll Community Telematics Ltd. ACT was set up in Lochgilphead at the beginning of 1992. It was decided that ACT would concentrate on three main IT activities: Computer Training, Offices Services and Teleworking. However in spite of an enthusiastic committee led by an influential and teleworking oriented Chairman, ACT failed to achieve any real prospect of viability. The writer is indebted to Peter Minshull (17) for this cautionary tale on the realities of setting up a telecottage.

On the training front, ACT set up a network of qualified trainers who lived locally to teach a range of computer courses. The trainees were charged a community rate and it was estimated that a minimum of five trainees would be required for a course to break even. The service was advertised through the usual local media channels. The response to this service was unsatisfactory and it would not have proved to be sustainable within the target timescale. This poor response was attributed to timing, competition, lack of ability to offer a recognised qualifiation coupled with the affluence and attitude of the local community.

The office services side consisted of the publicising of a fax receiving service and a basic design service for letterheads, menus and posters. A mailing list service was identified but not implemented. The services began to show some response during the Summer tourist season but did not build up sufficiently to indicate any real long-term sustainability.

Despite vigorous attempts at tendering for a number of European oriented Teleworking projects ACT discovered it did not have the internal organisation or skilled workforce to be considered capable of delivering the required standard of work. In other fields ACT proved to be very successful in identifying computer literate editors with a technical background for a project set up for a third party client. In doing so ACT found a vast resource of experienced and skilled people in its locality with the potential to benefit from teleworking.

The ACT report clearly highlighted some of the main problems in setting up a telecottage. It is often difficult to define the clear operation role for a telecottage and that role will depend on the nature of the community in which the cottage is located. There have to be serious doubts on the merit of providing limited public resources and funds to such in innovative concept as teleworking without a credible support service and unrealistic targets for self-sufficiency.

The ACT report concluded with four recommendations which are worth quoting in full:

- Identify each CTC's strengths and weaknesses in terms of available resources (both material and personnel, internal and external).

- Develop a critical mass of trained people in respective CTC locations.

- Network the CTCs.

- Provide professionally co-ordinated marketing support.

This cautionary tale does end on a high note. While the original CTC was closed down after one year of operation, it was replaced by a new, locally owned private company, imaginatively called ACT II Ltd. ACT II has already won a significant contract to provide secretarial services to a large firm of estate agents based in central Scotland.

THE EUROPEAN SCENE

The European Common Market, EEC, has for some time been anxious to encourage teleworking through a variety of schemes under the umbrella of ORA, (Opportunities for Rural Areas, Area 7 of the EC R & D programme on Telematic Systems). While half the population of the EEC live in rural areas, the quality of life and employment opportunities in these areas is under threat. In 1988 in its report on the future of rural society (18), the EEC Commission in Brussels realised that the new advances in telecommunications could help reduce the isolation of these areas. The Commission felt that the combination of advances in the fields of computing and telecoms or 'telematics' as it was called, could create or secure rural employment in the following ways (19):

– by the expansion of existing small enterprises in rural areas by giving them better access to markets;

– by enabling 'information intensive' enterprises to re-establish in rural areas;

– by stimulating the creation of services that can be provided from rural areas through new communications media;

– by enabling smaller manufacturing units to become viable through better communications with other companies in design, production and marketing activities.

The EC Commission invited project proposals for incorporation in the ORA workplan but limited funding meant that only 12 projects could be included in the first phase although over 50 proposals were submitted. Teleworking is not the primary concern of the ORA programme, it is designed to address the wider aspects of IT and Telecommunications in rural areas. The ORA projects of relevance to teleworking are, in the acronyms so beloved of the EEC, PATRA (Psychological Aspects of Teleworking in Rural Areas) and MITRE (Market Implementation of Teleworking in a Rural Environment).

There are other European teleworking initiatives being conducted under RACE II (R & D in Advanced Communications Technologies in Europe) programme. These include AGORA (A Great Opportunity for Rural Areas), APTITUDE (Advanced Platform Technologies in Teleworking for Underpinning a Decentralised Economy) and BARBARA (Broad Range of Community-based Telematic Applications in Rural Areas). It will be mid-1994 to 1995 before reports are produced for any of these projects. While the EEC certainly is committed to teleworking and ancilliary activities, particularly with regard to rural areas on the Communities periphery, its typically bureaucratic approach tends to suffocate rather than nurture. One delegate at an EC sponsored seminar on teleworking in Bonn was moved to comment that he felt that for every teleworker in Europe there were probably five academics or consultants studying him! Even in Britain there have been several feasibility studies commissioned for a cost that could have set up and run one telecottage for a year.

Most of the selection of international case histories quoted here have been drawn from a review of current practice conducted for the ORA scheme (20).

Denmark has been the most active European country with regard to telecottages but without much success. About 30 CTCs were set up in various villages, each featuring a café to help attract the locals to see what a CTC could do. Most of these CTCs failed due to a lack of community interest although a few were resurrected to concentrate on job-training for the unemployed. A notable exception to this Danish experience was the **Vejle Datariet CTC** which took the rural concept into an inner city environment. The Vejle CTC is extensively equipped with over 15 PCs, video and multimedia facilities and a crèche as well as the normal range of office equipment. After running for two years as a Government funded pilot scheme the Vejle CTC has now progressed to being a self-sufficient operation.

In France, telematics has been dominated by the tremendous success of its Videotext services, notably 'Minitel' which, with over three million installed terminals, is infinitely more popular than the equivalent 'Prestel' in Britain. Minitel is noted for its mass use by individuals encouraged by the French Government who have actively subsidised the service. France Telecom actively promote the service by offering to give you a Minitel terminal in exchange for your telephone directory!

While users of Minitel initially use the on-line directory enquiry service, they soon progress to using the wide range of other services on offer, most notably the range of teleshopping services offered by some of the French supermarket chains. Consequently there are very few CTCs in France and those that have been established have been funded by special interest groups.

There are estimated to be about 25 telecottages in the Republic of Ireland. While most are located in the Gaeltacht, the Gaelic speaking part of the country, they are spread from Donegal in the far north to Clear Island in the South-West. Most have concentrated in providing office and computer bureau services to their local communities. Funding has come from the EEC and a variety of national sources and they are expected to reach self-sufficiency within two to three years. But, as has been noted above in the case of ACT in Scotland, some are already experiencing conflict between community and commercial interests, especially when community funds have been involved.

There is a growing view in Ireland that perhaps the greatest contribution the telecottage could make to isolated communities will be in the field of education and distance learning. Ireland has many small offshore islands with no secondary education facilities and which are often cut off from the mainland in winter due to bad weather. Consequently, many children effectively leave their island at eleven or twelve years of age, never to return except for a holiday. As well as fulfilling its conventional role, a telecottage could also be configured for a modest extra cost as a centre for remote learning. Newfoundland has been a pioneer in this field with 40 remote learning centres linked by a Wide Area Network to the University in St. John's.

An interesting variation of the telecottage was set up in 1988 in the North West of Ireland, the Letterkenny IT Centre. It is located in a business park on the campus of the Regional Technical College. The centre's 'mission statement' stated that its objective was to be "the premier information and telecommunications systems facilitator in the North West of Ireland". The centre was seen as having a dual role, as a local catalyst for IT transfer and also as a provider of IT services to the public and private sector in the locality on a commercial basis. The intitial funding came from the EEC STAR (Special Telecommunication Action for Regional Development) programme and the International Fund for Ireland.

From its inception, the Letterkenny ITC concentrated on building up its revenue generating services which covered computer training, IT consultancy, software customisation and development as well as bureau and video-conferencing services. It has grown into a significant small enterprise in the area and currently employs 15 people with a wide variety of IT skills. By 1991 the centre's role as an catalyst for the dissemination of IT in the area was very much on the back burner and in danger of being dropped altogether when existing funding ceased.

Independent consultants, brought in to review the situation in 1991, reported that while the catalytic effect the centre had was going to be slow given the characteristics of the rural area in which it was located, funding for such a role was commercially justified. As a result, additional public funding will be provided for a further two years to specifically support the centre's catalytic role in the community. This study, by IBEX Consultants, would appear to be the only hard evidence available anywhere which confirms what is felt by many in the telecottage movement; namely that the telecottage concept has to be seen as a medium rather than a short-term strategy and that funding has to be structured accordingly.

American interest in CTCs has been muted compared with its interest in telecommuting and the satellite office (q.v.). However, pilot rural CTC schemes have been set up in Kentucky and Washington State.

The above examples give some indication of the varying character of telecottages worldwide, together with some of their problems especially in rural areas with a scattered and sometimes indifferent population. A large question mark hangs over the nature and conditions attached to start-up funding and ways must be found to reconcile community and commercial objectives. The case for the telecottage, in Britain at least, is not yet proven. There is also a danger, particularly in Europe, that the telecottage and to a lesser extent tele-working, will either get smothered in bureaucracy or studied to death by academics.

THE SATELLITE OFFICE

A Satellite Office is one whose transactions with the outside world are via its separate head or branch office and these transactions are conducted exclusively by telecommunication links. While satellite offices are rare in Britain they have been widely adopted elsewhere, notably in the USA. There, especially in California, teleworking is seen as having a major part to play in reducing traffic congestion and atmospheric pollution. It was estimated (21) that by 1990 there were over five million telecommuters in the USA and that several hundred major US companies had formally recognised telecommuting programmes for their employees. Satellite offices tend to be owned and operated by a single enterprise although there are some examples of shared facilities in the USA (q.v.).

As before, most of these case studies are culled from the ORA project review (20).

One of the earliest pilot telecommuter projects in the USA was started in 1985 by Pacific Bell, the State of California's largest PTT. Its objectives were twofold, to determine the benefits of telecommuting for the company and its employees and how its widespread adoption would affect the company's core business, telecommunications. Pacific Bell set up two satellite office suites, each catering for twelve employees, one in Los Angeles and one in San Fransciso. Each location was selected because it was close to the homes of the project's employees as well as being near to some of those employees' major customers. A detailed report of the project and analyses of the results can be obtained from Pacific Bell (22).

The Pacific Bell pilot scheme confirmed virtually every positive aspect of telecommuting, in that 96 percent of the participants in the scheme were satisfied with telecommuting.

A number of successful public sector telecommuting studies have been carried out in the USA, notably in Los Angeles and Hawaii. A combined public/private sector funded project has been piloted in the Los Angeles Area with the setting up of two 'Telebusiness Workcentres'. This project has been very successful with more applicants for space than can be accommodated. The role of the public sector to specify the objectives and to provide the initial seed capital to be matched by the private sector's contribution is now regarded as the standard approach. There is increasing evidence that the private sector will progressively meet the entire funding requirements for the concept as its benefits become ever more obvious.

Although most of the American moves towards satellite offices has been environmentally driven, there are many examples where the initiative has come from skill shortages or a need to cut operating costs. These satellite offices have not just been confined to mainland USA. The Republic of Ireland has seen over half a dozen American corporations' set up satellite offices, mainly in the west of the country. Set up costs are said to be 20 percent less than in the USA notwithstanding initial travel and airfreight costs, while competitive salaries in Eire are 60 percent of those in the USA. The Irish Development Agency (IDA) has been quick to exploit this new market and offers attractive incentive packages to American firms wishing to set up such information intensive operations. Other European countries have concentrated in attracting inward investment in only the manufacturing sector, so the Irish have had this lucrative niche very much to themselves.

The IDA has also paid considerable attention to the potential of higher added value opportunities in this sector and has not restricted its efforts to attracting fairly low-paid data input work, work which could eventually be transferred to even lower labour cost countries. A good example of this is the Software Development Centre established in Limerick by the Travelers Group of Companies, based in Connecticut. The Centre has its own dedicated link to the company headquarters in Hartford and employs around 30 Irish graduates to develop and maintain the software systems of the entire Travelers Group. As well as the obvious benefits from having a common language, the five hour time difference between the two locations works to advantage since a large part of the Irish working day is during the Connecticut night when computer activity in the Group is minimal.

In Switzerland, the bank Crédit Suisse set up a network of satellite offices to offset a chronic shortage of IT staff at its Zurich head office. From a standing start in 1985, Credit Suisse have now progressed to having eight satellite centres employing about 90, the numbers in each office varying from four to twenty two. The criteria for site selection were first, language (Switzerland has three official languages, French, German and Italian), secondly, the population of the catchment area and last the proximity of an existing CS branch. The last point was to facilitate the sharing of administration and infrastructure, it should be noted that the new satellite offices had a corporate function, working directly from the head office and had no contact with the bank's local customer base. Where possible CS started a satellite office by relocating a core team of IT staff from its headquarters in Zurich back to their home region.

The Crédit Suisse management carried out a survey of staff in the satellite and the findings were very positive on every count. Given the sensitive nature of much of the work together with the benefits of personal interaction in software development, they feel the dedicated satellite office is ideally suited to the bank's needs and far superior to teleworking from home or using a shared facility.

A notable example of a successful shared satellite office is the Jamaica Digiport facility at the Montego Bay Free Trade Zone. The Jamaica Digiport International was set up in 1988 as a joint venture operation between AT & T, Cable & Wireless and Telecommunications of Jamaica, the local PTT. The main objective of JDI was to help telecom's service companies in the free trade zone compete more effectively at less cost and to create more local employment.

The JDI is unusual in that its telecommunications links are centred round its own satellite earth station which utilises the Intelstat C-Band services. All JDI's traffic is with the USA and goes via a geo-stationary satellite to an Intelstat Earth Station in West Virginia. This link means that nearly all the value added telephone services that are available on the US mainland are available to JDI and it can be regarded as a remote extension to the AT & T network.

The JDI project is generally regarded as being very successful especially as it has led directly to the creation of 600 local jobs. However, the project has led to some controversy in the USA as it is perceived by some as the thin end of the wedge and the start of what could be an irreversible trend; the first example of the transfer of data-processing work to a developing country with much lower labour costs.

SUMMARY

Living as the writer does in a rural community, one cannot help but feel that the telecottage has a role to play in helping to revive depressed rural areas. However, the telecottage concept has some way to go to realise its full potential. In Britain in particular, community and commercial demands can make uneasy bedfellows and there is a need for a much more systematic and co-ordinated approach, perhaps on a national scale, than the various ad hoc schemes that have started thus far. But given what is to most people the highly innovative nature of the telecottage concept, it has to be looked on as a medium-term approach and it seems to be quite unrealistic to expect attitudes to change overnight. Present evidence suggests that one might get a better return by underwriting one telecottage for six or seven years than three telecottages for two years.

The Telecottage Movement itself will have to play a much more active role. It has to produce some convincing figures which will demonstrate that in terms of job creation and longterm economic benefit, the concept represents better value for money than competing infrastructural improvement schemes or the high-profile, mega-buck inward investment projects so beloved by National Enterprise Companies. There also has to be far greater effort put in to realising the potential of the personal computer as a teaching aid. At present, training is directed at the acquisition of computer and keyboard skills. With the advent of the CD-ROM, CD-I and Multimedia, the personal computer is beginning to deliver some of its potential as a medium for education. The telecottage is surely the ideal vehicle to bring this new technology to rural areas at least cost.

The case for the satellite office, whether as a base for telecommuting or as a way of compensating for skill shortages is well proven, although there has been little whole-hearted take up of the idea in Britain. It is important to appreciate that this facet of teleworking is all about job relocation and enhanced personal performance, not about job creation. It will be vital for the developed world to continuously upgrade the skills and job values of its IT dependent workforce and to be prepared for the inevitable when low-level data input jobs are transferred to a developing country such as Outer Pondoland where the locals will be only too delighted to do them for £2.00 per day. The writing is already on a wall in Montego Bay.

4 Working in the Home

In spite of what you may have heard to the contrary, working from home has never been a soft option. Having to cope with living in the shop, never mind above it, is not everyone's cup of tea. It requires considerable self-discipline on your part coupled with tolerance and co-operation on the part of your family. Unlike all the other occupations that are practised from home, teleworking is uniquely demanding in the quality of service expected. Indeed, one of its main selling features is that it should be completely 'transparent' to the client or employer. Therefore none of the little mistakes or rough edges that masquerade as 'rustic charm' in other fields will be tolerated in teleworkers.

It is essential for any potential homeworker to discuss their ideas with their partners and families at the earliest possible moment, and the budding teleworker is no exception. Two fundamentals of homeworking must be rigorously addressed at this preliminary stage; workspace, and family attitudes.

WORKSPACE

Not many forms of teleworking require an entire room to themselves, but most do require privacy if only to help one's concentration. If the teleworking also involves telephone calls, then privacy has to be backed up with sound proofing. It's difficult to sound professional on the 'phone when two infants are screaming their head off in the background.

Selection of workspace depends on the space and layout of one's home. Some are fortunate to already have a spare room, attic or basement that can be readily upgraded to a home office. Garages or garden sheds also have potential but do be careful with regard to (a) security, and (b) adequate heating. Computers and their accessories, never mind their owners, are particularly susceptible to dampness.

Where space is really at a premium, use your bedroom, after due consultation with your partner. It keeps your work space physically separate from your living space and a fully equipped electronic office can be readily accommodated in a fitted wardrobe. If you practise one-room living, try at least to arrange your workspace so it can be easily concealed, both for security reasons and to give you at least some relief from living cheek by jowl with your work.

FAMILY SUPPORT

Having dealt with the matter of workspace, the partner and other family members have to be taken into consideration. Whether they are infirm parents or relatives, toddlers, school children or students, their present and future needs have to be taken into account. Is teleworking being forced on the family unit by an employer, entered into as a potential source of a second income, or seen as a way of gaining employment without moving house? In each case the scenario will have to be thoroughly talked through.

To be successful, a teleworker is going to have to be totally professional and that attitude has to be respected by the rest of the household. Working in the home will introduce a range of new domestic pressures. Many women, and this is important since women traditionally are more likely to have keyboard skills than men, find that their husbands, partners and families will not take their work seriously; it's only for pin money, it's only for fun. Nothing could be further from the truth, and nothing can be so damaging to one's self-esteem. It is vital that as many as possible of the potential problems and flashpoints be recognised and rationally discussed by everyone before embarking on such an important new venture.

Men too can find that they can be under range of entirely new pressures when they take up teleworking. Friends and erstwhile colleagues may regard it as a 'cop-out' or soft option; an admission of failure to survive in the conventional commercial world. Wives and partners can suddenly resent having to share 'their' space during the day, and finds the working partner, even though they may be beavering away in a shed at the bottom of the garden or up in the attic, 'always under their feet', 'getting in the way' or else just cramping their social life.

These may look the flimsiest and most trivial of reasons on the written page. Yet all of us will be aware, to some extent at least, of how a domestic catastrophe can stem from an equally trivial incident or habit. Family life is a team game, and when the basic game, never mind the rules, is radically changed, it is essential that **all** the players are fully informed. Fortunately, society is becoming a good deal more flexible in its attitudes, but many old social conventions still persist. Just make sure that you and your team have worked out your tactics and covered most if not all the eventualities before you run out on to the field.

RULES AND REGULATIONS

Teleworking, like any other business run from home, is subject to a mass of rules and regulations. The most important of these cover planning permission, taxation, insurance, security and data protection, and last but not least, health and safety.

Premises

Planning law is administered by the local authority, (Regional Councils in Scotland) and requires you to apply for permission to change the use of your dwelling from residential to business use. While this may seem somewhat daunting, in practice what is meant is that the building or premises in question is not subject to 'Any Material Change of Use'. This is to ensure that a home is not used for any kind of work that is noisy, polluting, involves increased pedestrian or vehicular traffic, or anything else that might be incompatible with a residential area. Clearly this will not apply to teleworking, but local regulations must be checked and approval obtained in writing, to protect you from any future hassles.

Those of you with mortgages on your property will also have to inform the lender of the property's proposed change of use. Once again, teleworking is not likely to give rise to any objection, but it is essential to carry out this procedure and have the agreement in writing, especially as the lender often arranges the property's insurance. While computers, photocopiers and fax machines do not represent a known fire hazard, their presence in what is ostensibly a residence may negate insurance cover. By the same token, anyone living in rented premises will have to get permission from the local authority or landlord before commencing business.

Taxation and National Insurance

Some teleworkers will be full-time employees and taxed by the PAYE system. Full-time employment by teleworking is still in its infancy and contractual arrangements will have to be tailored to meet the needs of the employer and the employee. Special attention will have to be paid to matters such as timekeeping, pension rights, employer's liability insurance, custody and maintenance of any business equipment, and commercial confidentiality as well as the key area of remuneration. Company personnel and legal departments will no doubt draft out new forms of contracts of employment specifically for teleworkers, but in these formative stages it would be prudent to get an independent legal opinion before signing anything.

The majority of teleworkers are likely to be self-employed. The self-employed are taxed in a different way from those who are on PAYE, under what is known as Schedule D. This allows you to claim tax relief on many of your running expenses. You will have to appoint a chartered accountant, who will, for a fee (tax deductible), monitor your business account and submit the appropriate records to the local tax inspector. Find a practice that specialises in personal or small business accounting; if you don't know of one, ask around. Personal recommendation can be invaluable here. Given that, as a teleworker, you will be using a personal computer, consider buying a basic accounting programme such as 'Money Manager' to help you keep your financial records in order. Take your accountant's advice on the financial records he wants you to maintain, after all, it's what you're paying him for.

Pensions

Any change in employment status such as a move into teleworking is a good time to review one's pension arrangements. Some will already have their own personal and portable pensions. Others, changing from conventional employment to self-employment should certainly convert their Company Pension into a personal one. Take professional advice from a reputable broker and always shop around before making any decision. For those in the State Earnings Related Pension Scheme SERPS, it is probably prudent to wait a year or two after embarking as a self-employed teleworker before opting out and moving to a personal pension plan. Once again, if in doubt seek professional advice.

While not mandatory, it is strongly recommended that you open a business bank account. Although banks have had a lot of bad press recently, particularly with regard to their treatment of small businesses, do remember that they are in the business of lending money. Many have officials devoted entirely to the small business sector and can offer a great deal of (free) advice. What is vital in dealing with your bank is that you keep them totally informed of how your business is doing. Be realistic and always give them the bad news good and early. Bankers do not like nasty surprises and nothing makes them more nervous than a borrower who does not appear to be in complete control of his or her affairs.

It also makes good sense to set up a building society account expressly for your business. The self-employed pay income tax one year in arrears and it is a good discipline to put 25 percent of your income into such an account as you get paid. It gives you a more realistic idea of your actual income, it will earn a little interest and, if the worst comes to the worst, it can act as a reserve fund. Always remember that income tax has to be paid sooner or later.

VAT

All enterprises with annual sales in excess of £36,000 have to register with the Inland Revenue for value added tax. Most of the self-employed are unlikely to reach this threshold in their first year of operation, and the level is usually increased annually at the Budget. However, the situation must be monitored closely and the Inland Revenue do not take kindly to people who inform them retrospectively that they have exceeded the threshold. They like to have at least three months notice, so if you have any doubts, consult your local VAT office sooner rather than later.

Insurance

As indicated above, make sure any domestic insurance for both the fabric of your property as well as the contents are not invalidated by working from home. Consult a reputable insurance broker if you are in any doubt. Teleworkers should also consider additional permanent health insurance, to protect you if you are unable to work through illness or accident. You should also have Public liability insurance to cover any accidents when someone is on your premises or in your home in the course of business. Employers' liability insurance is compulsory if you employ anybody except your immediate family.

If your teleworking enterprise involves any kind of consultancy or the provision of any kind of professional advice, you will be well advised to consider some level of Professional Indemnity Insurance. This is expensive but protects you if someone sues you for having given them poor, if not downright bad advice. Many professional associations insist on their practitioners having this cover and can offer discounted schemes.

Health and Safety

Over the past few years the British Health and Safety Executive (HSE) and the office of the European Community have collected data in order to formulate a directive to provide reasonable protection for employees in a modern office environment without crippling businesses with excessive extra costs. The outcome is the EEC Directive 90/270, which will apply to all new offices opening on or after 1st January 1993, and to all existing offices from January 1997. The legislation should not be looked at as an expensive imposition on your enterprise. In practice, it is the formalisation of what are already regarded as good business practices, and in the context of teleworking are designed to benefit you, the user.

The main health hazard for computer keyboard operators is Repetitive Strain Injury (RSI). While RSI is a term which covers a variety of industrial maladies, with regard to keyboard operators the problem manifests itself in the muscles and tendons of the wrist, arm and neck. RSI develops progressively and results from long periods of keyboard work with the keyboard incorrectly positioned on the worksurface and the operator sitting with a bad posture. Personal computers must be on desks of the correct height and large enough so that the screen is not too close to the operator. The operator's chair must have adjustment for both height and back support. A number of foam rubber wrist rests are now available which can be placed in front of the keyboard to support the wrists and minimise strain.

Custom built computer workstations and operators chairs are available from most office furnishing specialists. Buying new can be expensive and many good second-hand bargains can be had through the small-ad columns of the local newspaper.

A further widely held health concern of computer operators is the radiation hazard from the VDU. This is dealt with in Chapter 9 on hardware.

The other main HSE requirement concerns office lighting which must be bright enough to obviate eyestrain but not so bright as to dazzle or cause undesirable reflections. A concise summary of the HSE requirements for office conditions is available from HMSO bookshops, and further advice can be obtained from any local office of the HSE.

Legal Advice

Nobody ever expects to become embroiled in litigation, in whatever shape or form. But to be forewarned is to be forearmed, and at least make introductory contact with a local solicitor. Quite apart from helping you through messy and potentially expensive 'hope not' situations such as defective goods or a broken contract, they can vet contracts of employment, and draft your own standard conditions of contract if required. Lawyer's fees might seem expensive but remember that their advice or skills may save you a great deal of worry and expense in the future, and they are tax deductible. Once again a local recommendation is best and be sure to check that the lawyer has experience with company law and small businesses. A solicitor who spends all his time conveyancing property and defending the local hooligans in court is not likely to be much use in the rough world of company litigation.

The Data Protection Act (1984)

This act is concerned with protecting the rights of the individual with regard to any information about them held on a computer. It sets out the principles of good practice which all organisations must observe in the collection, processing and disclosure of information about individuals. All organisations holding any data on individuals other than on that organisation's own payroll, must be registered with the Data Protection Agency. Further information on the Act can be obtained from HMSO bookshops or the Data Protection Registrar.

Data Security

The teleworker has to be aware that any kind of electronic data is susceptible to theft, corruption, loss, damage, and virus contamination. Data back-up systems may be required as well as protection against power failure or even fire. All too often many companies never mind individuals insisting on keeping their back up tapes, disks and whatever adjacent to the computer, and come a fire all is lost. All backups, be they of programmes or data must be kept in a physically separate building, the garden shed if necessary. Alternatively, fire safes are available but a good one, protecting records for up to two hours will leave little change out of £1000.

Depending on the nature and sensitivity of the data-processing work being carried out, it may be necessary to adopt certain security procedures when teleworking. The exact nature of these need not concern us at this stage; it is sufficient to be aware of the problem and its implications.

MISCELLANEOUS ADVICE

As well as the specific points mentioned above, it should be remembered that there are a large number of counselling, help services and training schemes available nationwide to the self-employed and small business enterprises. Sources of grant aid and start-up funds are dealt with in detail in Chapter 11. Public libraries and Citizens Advice Bureaux are good starting points to find out what is available, as are local councils, local development companies and training and enterprise companies. Finally, continually scan the national and local press for any snippets of information on new developments which might encourage or enhance your teleworking activity.

6 Marketing and Selling Teleworked Services

This is arguably the most important chapter in this book. More fledgling enterprises fail through a lack of marketing or marketing know-how than from any other single factor. In some cases, failure to understand marketing and the marketplace result in an innovative new enterprise being stillborn, its business plan failing to attract lending or venture capital.

Although the terms 'Sales & Marketing' are all too often used together, it is vital to understand that they are quite separate functions, and functions which require different personal skills. There are almost as many definitions of marketing as there are practitioners of the subject. They vary from the trite:

Selling goods that don't come back to customers who do to this formal and what is generally regarded as the definitive version from the Institute of Marketing itself:

Marketing is the management process of identifying, anticipating and satisfying customer requirements profitably.

A few people, the writer included, regard the failure to appreciate the true nature of marketing as the real British Disease, the root cause of our considerable industrial decline, rather than the traditionally accepted worker malaise. More often than not, in British enterprises large and small, 'marketing' is seen as a specialist function alongside line management, and thus has a subordinate role in the organisation. All too often in times of recession, an enterprise will react by reducing its overheads, an exercise which will include swinging cuts in its marketing department. Thus the enterprise immediately deprives itself of its best chance of getting out of its predicament. Perhaps the best one-liner on marketing, and one which neatly highlights its core function is from J. H. Davidson (23):

Marketing is an approach to business rather that a specialist discipline.

This emphasis on marketing is quite deliberate. Some of you may question its relevance to the self-employed. Others will find it daunting and off-putting; a discouragement to the many who may be thinking of embarking into teleworking, whether by branching out from one's current employer or by a change of career pattern and a desire to work from home. It should not be; it is largely a matter of common sense and doing one's homework. But it cannot be over-emphasised just how important this research and preparation is if you are to successfully move into the world of teleworking.

It is first essential to appreciate the kind of work that can and cannot be done by teleworking. At the present time it is probably easier to say what kind of work is not suitable for teleworking, occupations like shop assistants, production line workers, lorry drivers, pilots, doctors, nurses, law court officers, all of which require either hand or inter-personal skills. Some occupations are obvious candidates for teleworking, writers and journalists for example, many of whom were the pioneers of teleworking. Others which on the surface might seem ideally suited, such as computer programmers, in practice can turn out to be less so, since teleworking can deprive them of the personal interaction such as brainstorming which can often be the difference between success and failure in these fields.

A broad examination of the kinds of jobs that can be teleworked was undertaken in Chapter 1, while the various types of 'group' teleworking have been considered in Chapter 5. But remember that many other teleworking occupations have not yet been identified far less tried. Continuing advances in electronics and telecommunications will expand its sphere of influence and fundamentally challenge many of our society's basic tenets. Will, for example, schools as we know them exist in twenty years time? How long before the vast office building employing hundreds becomes a relic, a piece of industrial archaeology? This is not fantasy, it is technologically possible now; suffice it to say that the widespread adoption of teleworking will be restricted by human attitudes, not by technology.

Teleworking is likely to spread in two ways. One is 'from the top down' whereby senior management in an enterprise see that the adoption of one or more applications of the teleworking concept will improve their enterprise's performance, or, in these recessionary times, ensure its survival. The other is the reverse or 'from the bottom up' approach where potential teleworkers sell their services to existing businesses or organisations, the small as well as the large. Before considering each of these approaches in turn, the prospective teleworker should first carry out a thorough assessment of his or her personal expertise by way of a skills audit.

THE SKILLS AUDIT

Whatever the teleworker's underlying skill or profession, it is essential that he or she has at least a basic degree of computer literacy. This puts the distaff side at a considerable advantage as it is but a short step from typing to word processing. It is important to appreciate exactly what is meant by 'computer literacy'. In the teleworking context we mean the ability to effectively operate a personal computer in one or more of its main application areas; wordprocessing, spreadsheets, databases, graphics and so on. It should also mean having the ability to carry out what might be called the basic 'housekeeping' tasks of computing, communications (obviously), data back-up, file manipulation and so on. It does not mean the ability to write programs or be able to understand lines of computer program code.

Before taking steps to become computer literate budding teleworkers first have to assess their own personal skills and then consider how applicable they are to the concept of teleworking. If the outcome is in the affirmative, then, and only then, should anyone rush off to enrol on a computer training course. In assessing personal skills, one should always consider one's interests and activities outside one's employment. Look at your CV; if you haven't got one, now is as good a time as any to put one together. Accentuate the positive, play down the negative. But be honest; don't kid anyone and most of all, don't kid yourself. In today's competitive world, hands-on experience is often more relevant than a good honours degree. Many people have made dramatic and successful career changes in the past and teleworking can widen one's field of opportunity. Some may have toyed with the idea of studying for a degree with the Open University only to be put off by the fact that it would mean tearing up one's roots and moving in order to put the hard-earned degree to work. Teleworking might, for some, offer a way out of that dilemma, to be able to 'have your cake and eat it', as they say.

For the personal skills audit to be truly successful, one should always be mindful of the concept of Lateral Thinking, pioneered by Dr. Edward de Bono. It is impossible in a few words to do anything like justice to Dr. de Bono's far-reaching concept, but the principles can be illustrated by a couple of examples. For a teacher, is your most valuable skill your teaching ability or your knowledge of a specific subject? Might there be better scope either as a translator, if you are a modern language specialist, or in what will be a growing need for teaching skills in the as yet unexploited field of distance learning? Both applications lend themselves to teleworking.

Others who have been in some of the many fields of medicine or healthcare may find that their specialist skills will be relevant in compiling the new software for computerised management systems that will certainly be required by the new NHS Trusts. While there will never be a substitute for the person to person relationship in patient care, the whole gamut of medical skills will be necessary to compile and monitor the systems that will be needed by a modern health service and some of these will be most cost-effectively provided by teleworkers who have had hands-on medical experience.

While conducting a personal skills audit, you should be, subconsciously at least, constantly looking around as widely as possible for any opportunity where your skill and teleworking can fulfil a need, or where you believe there is an unexploited niche service which could be met by your skill, expertise and teleworking. As well as looking at companies and organisations do not overlook any services that might be required by other teleworkers, both in your locale and beyond.

Having by now ascertained that you have know-how and expertise which is appropriate to teleworking, you should now review the level, if any, of your computing skills. Many readers will already have a more than adequate level of computer literacy, so they should skip the next few paragraphs and move on to the next section.

Computing courses at differing levels are available from the various examination boards in schools in England, Wales and Scotland. Unfortunately the courses tend to be concerned with the fundamental principles of computing rather than giving students practical experience in the major software applications found in the real world. One therefore has to be careful to differentiate between training courses on computing as a subject and courses which teach one how to use a specific software package such as 'Wordperfect', 'MS Word for Windows' or 'Lotus 123'. The latter will be more relevant to the budding teleworker, although one should first find out which software packages are being used by your prospective clients. One notable exception to the generalist courses is the RSA course on Information Technology which is highly relevant to teleworking.

Information on computing courses in your area can be obtained from a number of sources such as schools, further education colleges, Training and Enterprises Companies, TECs, and so forth. Many course fees are subsidised and course times are often structured to suit the mature student.

More information on computer training is to be found at the end of Chapter 8 on Software.

In Britain, the only organisation currently representing the interests of teleworkers is the National Association of Teleworkers based in Bath, (see contact number in Appendix 2). This was only established this year and offers three categories of non voting membership; associate, corporate and educational. Associate membership at £46.94 seems very expensive for membership of what as yet is a 'not proven' organisation, and is reflected in the slow take-up; the Association had only four hundred members by the autumn of 1992. Fees for the corporate and educational sections are by negotiation.

IDENTIFYING OPPORTUNITIES

While this section is aimed primarily at prospective teleworkers who are not working in large organisations, it nevertheless has relevance to all prospective and practising teleworkers.

Some opportunities for teleworking have already been identified in Chapter 1. For those living in rural areas the biggest problem is the need to think globally while at the same time not overlooking any opportunities which may just lie over the hill. For teleworkers, it is largely academic whether your client is five or five thousand miles away; the principles are just the same. A Catch 22 for many rurally based teleworkers is how to carry out a market survey on a wide if not global scale, coupled with the problem of an individual pitching for business which if won would completely overwhelm said individual. Sound out the TECs, LECs, and local authorities to find out what, if anything they are doing about teleworking and have they identified other teleworkers and catalogued the skills available. Some might be persuaded to promote teleworkers in their areas on a local or national scale.

While it remains clear that a large part of British management is oblivious to teleworking and its benefits, it behoves the teleworkers to ensure that the world at large gets to know of their existence and what services they can offer. To this end, a national database service for teleworkers, The Teleservice Clearing House Ltd, (in which the writer has to declare an interest) has recently been established. This service offers teleworkers the opportunity to subscribe for a modest annual fee to a database which will progressively during 1994/95 be advertised in all 71 editions of the UK "Yellow Pages". Users will be able to search the database with up to four key criteria and have the printout faxed to them within half and hour. As well as this national service, there is ample scope for other small databases, specialising perhaps regionally or for a specific profession or skill. CTCs or telecottages would be ideal vehicles to provide such a service. Collecting the basic information need not be expensive; an advertisement in the local newspaper would reach most people, especially in country areas where readership of local papers is very high.

Some lists which identify the main occupational areas which are suitable for teleworking have already been given in Chapters 1 and 5. But as has already been pointed out, innovative uses of teleworking such as that of Crossaig Ltd. are comparatively rare, leaving a wide open field for the teleworking entrepreneur. Specialised information retrieval and the maintenance of Executive Information Systems, EIS, seem to be two notably fertile fields for teleworking activity. One should be constantly scanning the local and national press for any snippets of news which can offer teleworking opportunities. Speak to local business associations, Chambers of Commerce, TECs and LECs, further education colleges and so forth. Approach, if appropriate your professional association; are they aware of teleworking and have they considered its implications. Spread the word, for although teleworking is getting increasing coverage in the press, it is still very much a minority activity and any workshops and seminars on the topic tend to be talking shop with a good deal of preaching to the converted.

Finally, while it will depends on the skills a teleworker has to offer, do not on any account neglect the small business. Owner/managers are usually under constant pressure and frequently don't have enough time to come up out of the engine room on to the bridge to see where their ship is going. Various aspects of teleworking could provide them with cost-effective solutions to many of their problems. Take time to identify the ownermanagers in your area and find out if teleworking or even part-time use of your skills and your personal computer can be to your mutual benefit.

TAKING IT FROM THE TOP

The last decade has seen two major shifts in the basic attitude of many organisations and commercial enterprises. One has been the gradual realisation that the customer is king, and that catering to his, her or its needs and aspirations should be the focal point of every commercial entity. In Britain, this attitude is now beginning to permeate Government and we have recently seen the introduction of the Citizens' Charter, the Patients' Charter and so on. Put at its simplest, if you have no customers you have no business.

The other has been the growing appreciation that 'quality' whatever that means to each and every organisation or enterprise has to be 'built in', an integral part of an organisation's structure and culture, not just a bolt-on accessory. This concept was first elucidated in the USA in the 1950s by Dr. W. Edwards Deming. Like many original thinkers, Deming was a prophet without honour in his own country; his ideas found little support in corporate America. Undeterred, Deming took his proposals to Japan where they found wide acceptance and are regarded as having been one of the key components in that country's economic resurgence and its conquest of many Western markets. Deming's ideas are commonly referred to as the concept of "total quality management" (TQM).

These two fundamentals should be the foundation of every prospective teleworkers' approach to marketing and selling their services. The 'Top Down' approach can work in two ways. A manager can convince his superiors that teleworking can enhance his performance and hence that of his company's, and/or, the manager demonstrates that adoption of teleworking in one or more of a company's departments will improve its performance. This improvement may be from cost savings, greater efficiencies, a better service for customers or a combination of all three.

How this is done will depend on the manager, his or her position in the organisation and the nature of the organisation. A very comprehensive and persuasive approach to selling teleworking from within an organisation, is given in the Mercury Communications Ltd. publication 'The Teleworker Portfolio'. Above all, it repeatedly emphasises the importance of relating any proposals to the needs of the organisation, not to extolling the virtues of teleworking.

To paraphrase the salient features of the Mercury approach, first emphasise the benefits teleworking can bring to some of the key issues in your organisation. Recruit a powerful ally at the top of the organisation to champion your cause. Bring in others at the earliest stages of the project; create a teleworking team and ensure that you use all the available experience from within the organisation. Present a well thought out formal proposal to set up a pilot teleworking scheme, and clearly establish the criteria on which the success of pilot project will be judged. The object of the pilot scheme should be to demonstrate the feasibility of teleworking in your organisation.

Notwithstanding the validity of such an approach, it must always be borne in mind that selling some of the virtues of teleworking to any organisation can be a severe test of diplomacy if it is to prove successful. The concept of teleworking and the realisation of just what can now be achieved by remote working often challenges some of the basic tenets of conventional office practice and the classic organisational structure. Many in middle management will quickly see teleworking as a serious threat to their very existence in any new scheme of things. Thus the proponents of teleworking, if they are to be successful, will have to carefully think through their ideas and to fully appreciate the knock-on effects of their proposals before going public. They should also be uncommonly careful in how they garner their in-company support.

Within any organisation there will be many who will thrive on the responsibility and freedom that teleworking can offer. But a word of caution. Teleworking imposes a whole new set of personal requirements, notably self-reliance and self-discipline quite apart from the need for domestic space and stability highlighted in the previous chapter. Thus the selection of potential teleworkers will involve the consideration of an additional set of personal parameters from that used in the selection of someone for a conventional office-bound job. As yet, no one appears to have drawn a personality profile for the perfect teleworker. Until then, the personnel professionals will have to play it by ear while teleworking becomes much more widely adopted.

FROM THE GROUND UP

Whether one is approaching a prospective client or company as a individual teleworker or offering a new kind of service through teleworking, it is imperative when planning your presentation to put the potential customers needs above all others. The customer has to benefit in one way or another from the service on offer, and he or she will have to be convinced that using the service is to **their** advantage not that of the teleworker. It is up to the individual teleworker to identify what the advantages might be for each potential customer; that is the essence of marketing.

The first stage, having identified your own teleworking skills from the skills audit procedure is to conduct a preliminary matching of those skills to a theoretical company profile. For those with secretarial or book-keeping skills that might seem very straightforward but remember that to be a teleworker you have to identify companies who are already using personal computers even if they are not yet 'au fait' with modems and electronic data transfer or at the leading edge of IT. A first trawl for suitable companies in your vicinity can be carried out using the 'Yellow Pages'. Continual use of the local and national press has already been mentioned as an invaluable source of information. Look for items on companies who have won new contracts, who are expanding or who are moving into new products as well as anything on changes in local government services or organisation. Review each news item carefully and consider how they might give you an opportunity to provide a service by teleworking.

It is often difficult to identify the key person in the organisation, the one who makes the decisions. Many companies have sophisticated systems in place to confuse the unsuspecting salesperson. While all purchasing decisions may be approved at board level, they probably rubber-stamp the requisition made by a much lower form of managerial life whom the salesperson has to try and identify. In some companies it will pay to contact the computer services manager, in others it will require an approach to a director or perhaps even the chairman since the adoption of teleworking can have far-reaching consequences. Visit your local library and look through the trade directories to be found in the reference section. Many of these will identify all the company officers and a few tactful phone calls should enable you to identify your objective. Local authorities are bound by law to make available the names of all their officials.

Finally, at the risk of repetition, always remember that to be successful you have to identify a service which will benefit the consumer or client. In addition, what you are offering has to provide the potential customer with some sort of competitive advantage. Whatever it is, it will have to be something that is easier, cheaper, quicker, faster, better, or newer than current practice. It might even be that rarest of rarities, something unique, but to succeed its benefits will still have to be seen to percolate down to the bottom line.

SELLING TELEWORKING

Now we really come to the nitty gritty. You've done your market research, identified the key person in an appropriate company and made the appointment. "How on earth," you think to yourself, "can I sell perhaps £15,000 of teleworking to a hardened business executive?" Do not despair, almost everyone has some selling ability. After all, most of us, consciously or otherwise, spend at least some of the time trying to sell our ideas, aims and objectives to others, no doubt with varying degrees of success. The prospective teleworker has the advantage that unlike the average salesperson they will be selling a service rather than an expensive capital goods item.

This section is not about how to become a super-salesperson in only two months, although there are a number of specialised books available for the professional salesperson which do, and in considerable detail. We are going to consider only the fundamentals of the selling process and these can be paraphrased into what might be called the five P's of selling:

- Be Prepared
- Be Professional
- Be Presentable
- Be Punctual
- Be Polite

And, with due respect to the Gospels, the greatest of these is preparation.

All of us at sometime will have been faced by a truly silver-tongued sales professional. Whatever product or service was being sold we found ourselves being unconsciously swept along, agreeing with this and accepting that until it was we ourselves who told the salesperson that we wanted to buy whatever was on offer. We were blissfully unaware that we had been sold anything; we had just made a particularly sound investment. Such a sales technique is the result of years of practice and a lot of hard work, often based on learning many different standard approaches by rote. This section aims to show how even the most gauche can make an effective sales pitch and win for themselves a slice of the teleworking market.

The importance of thorough preparation cannot be overstated. In our case it is a combination of market research and plain old-fashioned homework. In sales parlance, market research is known 'qualifying' and any sales professional will tell you that the more qualified the prospect the easier it is to make a sale. The essentials of market research have been covered earlier in this Chapter, but always remember that no matter how thorough and up to date you think this has been, you will not know everything about your prospective client or his aspirations. When drafting out your presentation always allow for the unexpected and don't paint yourself into a corner.

While most of us would regard speech as the vital tool in the selling process, one must never underestimate the use of the other senses. As soon as you are introduced to your prospective client look straight at them and quickly establish eye contact. It is also essential in any sales presentation to periodically shut up and listen, usually more often than one might think necessary, to what the prospective client is saying. The voice itself is very much a double-edged weapon. Both in tone and content it can be a help or a hindrance. If you do try to be humorous to lighten the situation, it must be at your expense; never, never at the client's. Try to appear confident without being brash, and try to hide at least some of the inevitable nervous tension.

One of the simplest and most effective techniques of the sales professional is to ask questions that avoid a yes or no answer. For one thing they keep your presentation moving along, when a bald "no" can stop you dead in your tracks. Secondly, they can help you learn even more about your prospective client's operation. For example, rather than ask "Does your company find personal computers and computerisation useful?" try "Which type of personal computers do you use, IBM PCs or Apple Macs?" With the latter question you have kept things moving along **and** at the same time learnt what computing platform they use. Even if the answer is neither, it will almost always tell you what is being used. "Actually we use AX400s running OS/400" It can be very useful for pinning down that elusive appointment; "I would like to arrange to have half an hour of your time Mr. Smith; would Tuesday morning or Thursday afternoon be more suitable?" But do make sure that your sales pitch does not over-run the half hour slot you obtained. The alternative answer/question can be a very powerful technique but it takes a lot of careful thought to put a series of suitable questions together to fit your own personal style and presentation, while accommodating the various combinations of answers.

One of the greatest difficulties for the sales tyro is how to overcome the perennial problem of questions and objections. Both should be seen as ways of enhancing your presentation and improving the quality of your market research. If you respond to the question, "Can you have this service up and running in four weeks?" with a simple "Absolutely no problem, Mr. Jones", you have gained nothing. If, on the other hand, your reply "Is starting on the fifteenth of next month the best time to meet your company's requirements", Mr. Jones is almost duty bound to accept your proposal.

Virtually every product or service that is being offered for sale is susceptible to varying degrees of objection. The sales professionals soon learn the run of the mill objections to their product or service and prepare their responses in advance. They don't lose out to objections, they are successful because they know how to handle them. To be fair they will have had many more opportunities than the budding teleworker will want to have hearing about them, so in our case we shall have to take time to be devil's advocate and try to suss them out for ourselves and then formulate our responses beforehand.

All of us can be reluctant purchasers and the business executive is no exception. Some minor objections are merely a defence mechanism, a way of slowing things down. Others are a coded method by which the prospective client can find out more about the product or service. Major objections can sometimes turn out to be what is known in the trade as a condition. A condition is a legitimate reason for not proceeding with sale. A condition cannot be overcome, a fact that has to be accepted as gracefully as possible.

Without doubt it takes a great deal of practice to become truly skilled at fielding awkward questions, but a few points should set you along the right path. First, listen carefully and hear the question out attentively and courteously. Don't jump down the client's throat as soon as he's got half a dozen words out. Secondly, practice a technique used by virtually every politician on television; repeat the question back to the questioner. It confirms that you have really heard the question while giving you a little time to think out your reply. If the question is a real googly, strange as it may seem it can pay to question the question. This has to be done with diplomacy, carefully and conscientiously and without the slightest hint of superiority or, even worse, sarcasm. As your prospective client further explains his objection, you have some more time to prepare your reply, but not at the expense of listening to what is being said. Last, answer the objection directly. Obviously this is easier said than done but it never pays to be evasive. Everything has its strengths and weaknesses but consider offsetting the weakness by accentuating a positive attribute. "Lack of supervision is a concern Mr Black, but you will of course be reading every letter and document I produce before you sign them". Or, in a different situation, "Yes, of course your telephone charges will increase, but you will not have to increase your overheads while at the same time you will be providing a far superior customer service".

For the would-be teleworker, given that the adoption of teleworking is likely to represent a major shift in attitude if not in policy, an all too common conclusion to a sales pitch will be something along the lines of "I'll think it over", "I'll have to discuss this with my board/colleagues/partner", "Why don't you come back to me at the end of the week", etc., etc., etc. There are no cut and dried answers to this one. The first response is to confirm quite slowly and carefully that the client is going to think it over. Deliberately ask if there are any other features the prospect does not understand or is uncomfortable about. If you have time, quickly recap the salient features of the proposal and make a dignified withdrawal.

It is a good idea to use a shorthand pad in a sales meeting. You can write your prompt notes on the top half of the page and have space for your own notes as the meeting proceeds.

You will have to learn to accept some rejection and failure. Look on rejection as an emotionally painful but necessary part of the learning curve.

Conduct a realistic post mortem on your failures; unless one is very insensitive one can usually pinpoint the moment when it all started to go wrong. We are all pretty good at realising a moment or two later what we should have said. Make notes as soon as you can after every meeting and incorporate everything you have learned into refining your presentation. Learning some kind of script off by heart is not recommended for the beginner, as any deviation from said script can leave you floundering. It is much better to act out some basic scenarios which will allow some flexibility with a tolerant friend or partner.

It is to be hoped this emphasis on the preparation of a sales presentation is taken in a constructive way. The objective has been to maximise the effect of every sales pitch as it is assumed that most readers would rather be teleworking than selling.

The prospective teleworker has to be totally professional. It has already been stated that for teleworking to be successful it has to be virtually transparent, and all the little faults and glitches which can masquerade as rustic charm in other fields will not be tolerated. No one should ever try to sell teleworking per se; teleworking is only the means by which the service you are offering is delivered. Thus while one must have all the technical jargon and answers about teleworking at your fingertips during a sales presentation, never ever lose sight of the service you are offering and the need to demonstrate your own mastery of the subject. Lurking at the back of almost every business executive's mind is the feeling that using teleworkers will somehow equate to a loss, a loss of control, of quality, of an indefinable something they often cannot put a finger on. After all, they are being asked to relinquish a corporate activity to a comparative if not complete stranger who, when they start working, may not even be seen for what might be months on end. That is a pretty tall order and one that can only be overcome by someone exuding confidence and professional competence.

Appearance plays a vital role in helping to establish the right impression. Your prospect is not in the slightest bit interested in whether you run a croft in your spare time, but he or she will be far from impressed if you turn up for a meeting looking as though you have just finished mucking out the cowshed. Be presentable; conventional management wisdom equates a slovenly appearance to slovenly work. Notwithstanding the vagaries of fashion, personal grooming and appearance do matter and one should never underestimate the impact of that all important first impression.

Business executives are busy people and their time is precious, to them at least. As a result, nothing is more likely to get a sales presentation off on the wrong foot than for you to arrive, harassed, puffing and blowing twenty minutes after the appointed time. Your prospective client will be annoyed before you have even begun, you yourself will be in no fit state to carry out an effective presentation and you will have lost most of your allotted time, unless of course you wish to incur even more executive wrath by over-running your time slot.

Punctuality is a most basic business courtesy, quite apart from being a further demonstration of your professional approach. First, find out exactly where you have to go; if necessary phone the company switchboard to ask for explicit directions after you have made the appointment. Think ahead, if public transport or long distances are involved, don't make appointments for nine o'clock in the morning. The prospective teleworker is unlikely to have more than two appointments in one day so you should try to get to the immediate vicinity at least one hour before the appointed time. It will give you time to have a coffee, relax a little and to go over your notes. Always set off and allow plenty of time to cope with the unexpected, be it a puncture, a motorway pile-up or even a bomb threat.

Try to arrive at the venue ten minutes before the appointed time. Reception will inform your prospective client of your arrival and you will have a few more minutes to get your mind into top gear. If the worst comes to the worst and you find that you are going to be late, even slightly late, make plans to be able to phone ahead well before the appointed hour to inform the company of your problem. If, on the other hand, you are kept waiting, you will just have to suffer in silence. Remember that two blacks do not make a white.

"Please" and "thank you" are probably the most important yet underutilised words in the business vocabulary. These days it sometimes appears that the 'macho' approach to personal relations is de rigeur and that civility is a sign of weakness, of being a soft touch. Don't believe it. Courtesy costs you nothing and can reap handsome dividends. For all you know, the frosty lady behind the reception desk might be the chairman's secretary whose views carry considerable weight. A brief smile and a pleasant "Good Afternoon, I'm . . ." can soften the wintriest countenance. A few pleasantries about the decor, the weather or how clear were your directions never go amiss, but don't go overboard. Very often a prospective client will ask his staff what they thought of you after you have left and they will not be impressed by either a cocksure or overly obsequious attitude. Above all, never, never allow yourself to be drawn into an argument. No matter how sure you may be of your facts, arguments are to be avoided at all costs. If the customer is always right, be assured that a potential customer is even more right!

Courtesy should of course extend to your correspondence. Always write and confirm any appointment you have made and always write and thank a prospect for his time and attention after every meeting, irrespective of the outcome. If appropriate, confirm that you are looking forward to the decision they promised you, and remind them to call you if they have any more questions. There is no need to be to flowery and effusive, a brief word of thanks and appreciation are all that is necessary and they will then have your name on file.

In concluding this chapter, one should remember that the euphoria that will always surround a successful sale should be tempered with the realisation that the selling was in fact the easy bit; now you are going to have to deliver what has been promised, and that could well be a good deal harder.

7 The Software

INTRODUCTION

Having attempted to keep this book as clear and non-technical as possible, we have at last come to the stage where we have to introduce the prospective teleworker to at least a modicum of technical jargon. It should be clear to any prospective teleworker reading this book that the personal computer is the cornerstone by which teleworking is provided or delivered. Being an effective and competent teleworker does not usually require a deep and thorough understanding of electronics or computer programming. What is needed is a good grasp of both the capabilities and limitations of the application software being used together with a sound knowledge of what might be called the 'housekeeping' of a personal computer system.

This and the next chapter take the budding teleworker through what many might regard as the technological maze of personal computing. This chapter starts by describing the various operating systems used by the three main types of personal computers. The 'operating system' is a core program that translates the instructions from the various application programs and converts them into signals that can be understood and acted upon the computer's central processing unit. It then goes on to describe the main categories of application programs, their purposes and limitations.

In a similar way, Chapter 8 takes the reader through the essential components of a personal computer and its associated peripheral devices, explaining both what they do and how they affect the performance of a personal computer system as a whole.

Computer jargon is littered with acronyms designed to confuse the uninitiated. Throughout this book, when an acronym is introduced, the full name is used followed by the acronym in parenthesis. Thereafter the acronym alone is used. For anyone who may get lost, all acronyms and technical terms that are used in the text are fully explained in the Glossary at the end of the book.

Most people, and more than a few companies, buy their computer in quite the wrong way. They select a machine they like, sometimes after a brief demonstration, pick up a bundle of software and take it all home. More often than not they fail to take the necessary time to learn how the computer and its programs work, then quickly lose interest and it is all consigned to a dusty corner.

Logically, one should start by sitting down and deciding exactly what one wants the computer to do. Is it word processing, book-keeping, desktop publishing (DTP), financial analysis, graphical design and so forth? Next, one looks for a program or suite of programs that will do the work to your satisfaction. Do not make your decision by simply reading through all the glossy brochures produced by the software companies; do try and get a hands-on demonstration. Failing that, read up the 'road tests' of software published in the computer magazines. Only after you have selected the appropriate program or programs does one look for a suitable computer on which to run the programs.

Inevitably things are never quite as simple as that, especially for the prospective teleworker. There is more than one type of 'personal computer'; with regard to the UK there is IBM PC and Apple Macintosh in general business use, the Acorn/Archimedes in education and the rest nowhere, at least from the standpoint of teleworking. There are also 'workstations' but their use is restricted to the rarefied atmosphere of computer aided design (CAD), and need not concern us for now. The issue is further complicated by the fact that Apple Macintosh computers, while outnumbered in Britain by about seven to one are totally dominant in the fields of desktop publishing and printing, and very strong in architecture. Above all, the budding teleworker has to be mindful of the need for compatibility in his or her chosen field of work.

Throughout this section the watchword is 'compatibility'. If you are going to telework for your present employer you will already know what systems and programs are in use. For others, it makes sense to wait until you know for whom you will be working before buying. This may be impractical if you need to get some training before launching yourself at the marketplace. In this case go for one of the market leaders in a specific category; many of the leading brands have an import–export capability with their rival programs.

Most importantly, do not succumb to saving money by using a pirated copy of a well-known program. First it's illegal. Secondly, it's a common way of letting a 'virus' into your system. Thirdly, and especially relevant to the teleworker; you will not be able to take advantage of the 'helpline' service offered by many of the leading software companies if you have a problem. They will soon find out if you are not a legitimate user and this could lead to prosecution. Last, with a legitimate purchase you will usually get an inexpensive opportunity to upgrade, thus keeping your application programs up to date. For the self-employed, software purchases will be tax deductible.

One final point before we get into the meat of this section; operating systems and application programs are continually being upgraded. They come in versions, numbered 1.0, 3.1, 4.2 and so on. The unit number refers to a major change, with many new facilities. The number after the decimal point refers to minor changes and very often is to remedy bugs and glitches that have become apparent after a major program re-vamp. Software companies are undoubtedly guilty of shipping programs out to an eagerly waiting market before they are fully tried and tested.

OPERATING SYSTEMS

The Operating System is the core program in any computer. It is started the moment a computer is switched on and basically it translates an application program into instructions that are recognised by the computer's processor. With Apple and Acorn/Archimedes computers the operating system is specific to that brand of computer and comes packaged with it. With the IBM PC and its clones, while each computer will come complete with an operating system, there is a choice and the operating system can be changed to suit the users' needs. The common operating systems for the IBM PC and its clones are MS-DOS, DR-DOS, OS/2, UNIX, and a hybrid, the widely known 'MS Windows'.

When operating systems such as DOS and UNIX were first compiled, computers were operated exclusively by specialists with a thorough understanding of computers and computer programming. As a result, most of today's millions of PC users still have to struggle, at least some of the time, with an operating system's strange command instructions and its hypersensitive grammar or syntax as it is more correctly known. The history of the development of operating systems is convoluted and what follows is an outline of the essential written, hopefully, in easy to understand form.

History

The original DOS was written in the late seventies by a company called Seattle Computers who then sold it to a company called Microsoft run by a young man called Bill Gates. Microsoft's own programmers completely revised DOS to produce what was called MS-DOS 2. In what must go down as one of the deals of the century, Gates convinced IBM to offer MS-DOS with their new ranges of desktop computers called Personal Computers. Originally, four different kinds of DOS were offered by IBM but in a very short time MS-DOS had emerged the clear winner. This was the foundation of the Microsoft company's extraordinary success and MS-DOS has continuously been improved and updated through the years to the current version, 5.0.

In 1984 Apple Computer introduced the first 'Macintosh' computer with its revolutionary Graphical User Interface (GUI). Moving a desk-top device known as a Mouse, moved a pointer on the screen of the VDU; move the mouse to the left and the pointer moves left, move it away from you and the pointer moves up the screen and so on. The various commands were represented on the screen by symbols known as Icons. Using the mouse to move the pointer to an icon and clicking one of two buttons on the mouse initiated the command or could start a programme. This was much easier than typing in, what was to many, gobbledegook from the keyboard.

This breakthrough did not bring Apple all the commercial rewards it might have expected (see p) but it forced Microsoft to see how it developed a similar system for the IBM PC. A feature of the IBM PC from the start was that all future developments both in programs and processing power were 'backwards compatible'. That is to say that all applications will run on each generation of PC, but they will run more slowly or handle less data on early machines compared with the latest model. Microsoft's solution was to devise 'MS Windows' which was an add-on operating system running 'on top of DOS' as it were. 'Windows' used similar GUIs and a mouse to the Apple Mac and was also able to take advantage of the newly available processing power to meet what had become an increasing need, particularly in the fields of graphics and DTP, multi-tasking, the ability to run more than one program at a time.

Windows Software

The early versions of 'Windows' were not very successful but all that changed in the spring of 1990 with the launch of 'Windows 3.0'. Sales took off, more than 6 million copies being sold in two years. Version 3.1 came out in the spring of 1992 and has a number of significant improvements over version 3.0 but is not yet perfect. Most users will at some time have come across 'Windows'' unique and catastrophic Unrecoverable Application Error (UAE) message which indicates the total loss of what can be many hours work. Nevertheless 'Windows' is here to stay and an increasing number of applications programs can now run on the Windows platform.

Apart from UAE, 'Windows'' main disadvantage is that it and its programs take up very large amounts of computer memory both to store and run them. While Microsoft recommend a minimum of 2 Megabytes of RAM, 4 Megabytes is essential for reasonable performance. As for hard disk capacity, get as much as you can afford.

OS/2 is different in that it is a stand-alone operating system with GUI and multi-tasking capability. It has now progressed to version 2.0, and it will reputedly run DOS applications better than DOS itself. This most recent version has received much criticism and it is not regarded as being sufficiently ready or user-friendly for a computer novice.

There is another, highly specialised operating system for the PC, UNIX. This is an open but specialised system needing at least a 386 processor and whose main strength lies in its ability to let PCs communicate with mini-computers. UNIX requires a large amount of storage space and has to be installed by specialist. The main UNIX distributor in the UK is the Santa Cruz Operation.

For the IBM PC and its look-alikes, the choices are as follows. For a plain, no frills DOS there the choice of MS-DOS, now up to version 5.0 by Microsoft and DR-DOS, version 6.0 by Digital Research. There is little to choose between them in either capability or price. For a GUI and multi-tasking facility the choice is between 'Windows 3.1' running on, ideally, MS-DOS 5.0 or the stand-alone OS/2 2.0. At present 'Windows' is the better bet; however if you can afford to wait, Microsoft will be introducing its new stand-alone operating system 'Windows/NT' (New Technology) early in 1993. It promises to be everything that 'Windows 3.1' *should* be and more.

WORD PROCESSING

It has been said that over 90 per cent of all personal computers run word processing software some of the time. It is perhaps the one computer application where the benefits are immediately visible; beautifully presented, error-free letters and documents. Not surprisingly, such widespread use has spawned an equally wide variety of programs, from very simple text editors to all singing, all dancing packages whose capabilities approach the standards of desktop publishing.

Choosing a word processing package requires a detailed analysis of your requirements together with some idea of how an individual works and how much or how little appears on the screen. All word processing packages can carry out a range of basic tasks; word-wrap, insert and delete, search and replace, mail merge, spell checkers and so forth. It must have adequate printer support, e.g. does it have to support laser printers with multiple fonts and proportional spacing of text? What is the precise nature of the application? Does it entail the use of imported or embedded graphics, complicated tables or complex mathematical or scientific notation? Will a sophisticated mail merge facility be required? Other users will require a 'style sheet' facility which makes it possible to create a range of documents to suit a particular corporate or house style.

Many of the top level word processing programs have features that will only be used in a few specialised circumstances. The average user is unlikely to explore many of the more exotic realms of word processing such as revision tracking or file linking to other applications. However, for the teleworker, an electronic mail facility should be regarded as a 'must'.

Once the essential capabilities have been decided, final selection will often be a matter of personal taste, notably in regard to what you see on the VDU. Do you really need true WYSIWYG (what you see is what you get) or will a rougher 'print preview' suffice. Some people like to see all the tabs and formatting codes as they go along; others prefer to keep the writing and formatting separate. Some prefer pull-down menus others a plain uncluttered screen. All things are possible, well, nearly all. One word of caution; it is widely agreed that the first word processing programme one learns sticks indelibly in the mind. You have been warned.

In the UK, WordPerfect 5.1 is the clear market leader in DOS-based word processors with 50 per cent of the market. Microsoft 'Word for Windows 2.0' is the leading Windows-based package. For the Apple Mac, Word 4.0 is the leader, while EasiWriter is a leading package for the Acorn/Archimedes.

It is also worth noting that while a number of top-end packages have a translation ability and can import and export files to a number of other word processing programs, purposed designed translators such as 'Word for Word' are available.

SPREADSHEETS

A computerised spreadsheet is a program which manages grids of small boxes called cells into which numbers, text or formulae are inserted. A complete grid of cells is called a worksheet. The powerful and time-saving feature of spreadsheets is that when the contents of any cell are changed, the values in all the other cells depending on that cell are instantly recalculated. It is this ability that is one of the spreadsheets most powerful attributes, particularly for financial predictions - the 'What if?' calculation.

The first spreadsheet programme VisiCalc came out in 1979 and was hailed at the time as the most useful computer program ever devised. Undoubtedly accountants and financiers were the first to appreciate the power of the concept for budgeting, cashflow prediction and investment decisions. The spreadsheet's other great strength is its flexibility which allows virtually unlimited variations in its use. It can, at a push, serve as a basic database and even a word processor.

The spreadsheet has come a long way since VisiCalc was introduced. Graphing, the ability to construct several types of graph or chart from data contained in the spreadsheet, import–export features and some degree of WYSIWYG are now widely accepted as the norm. Over time, unofficial standards have become adopted based largely on the hugely successful Lotus 123 package, and most of its rivals can use worksheets in the 123 format. A further important development has been the three dimensional or 3-D spreadsheet whereby a cell in one worksheet relates to a cell in another which can be very useful in compiling interrelated financial statements. This 3-D capability must not be confused with the ability of a program to produce 3-D type graphs and charts.

Spreadsheets have one notable weak spot. They all use what might be called a mini programming technique called a 'macro'. A macro, in its most basic form, is a way of automating a frequently used sequence of keystrokes. Macros can be used to automatically specify the currency, bank rate, and whether time interval is weekly, monthly or quarterly. The problem can occur when the person compiling the macro makes an un-noticed error, not as unlikely as one might think since spreadsheets are rarely constructed by people with a good grounding in computer programming. The results can vary from the bizarre to the financially crippling.

Be sure to pay attention to printer output of spreadsheet programs. Most worksheets are long and shallow and so must be printed out down rather than across an A4 sheet of paper. This is not a problem with laser and bubble-jet printers, but can pose difficulties with dot-matrix printers. If the selected package does not have this facility, you can buy an add-on program, such as 'Sideways'.

Lotus 123 has been for many years a leading spreadsheet package and versions are available for both DOS and 'Windows' platforms. Recently Microsoft's Excel has become the leading 'Windows package'. Variants of Lotus 123 and Excel are also available for the Apple Mac. PipeDream 3 is a leading spreadsheet program for the Acorn/Archimedes range.

DATABASES

The database was one of the earliest uses of the computer in business, one punched card being one database record. Many of what seem at first sight to be imaginative computer applications turn out to be no more than the novel use of databases. Consequently there is a very wide variety of packages available in this sector. They vary from a simple database provision as part of a utilities package, to the most esoteric, such as Clipper 5.0 from Nantucket which is little more than a kit of parts for the professional computer programmer. Thus while database input and manipulation are areas with great potential for the teleworker, the actual package should not be selected until one knows *exactly* what the client or employer wants or what package they use.

Databases come in two distinct flavours; the 'flat file' database and the 'relational' database. All databases hold their 'records' in what are known as 'tables'. Each record will have a number of 'fields', one for each piece of information held by the record. This information may be character based, e.g. first name, last name; number based, e.g. cost, quantity; date/time based and a fourth category, 'logicals' which mean simply conditions to which the answer is yes or no. A further variation on some packages is the provision of 'choice', e.g. marital status can be single, married, separated, divorced or widowed. A database can have one or many tables, but the key difference between the two main types is that a flat file system can only use one table at a time while a relational database can use several, with at least one 'key' field being common to each.

The power of the database is in its speed in answering all manner of questions regarding the records in the tables. For example, how may widgets were sold in the second quarter of this year; how many customers purchases are over £100, what were our average sales to candlestick makers in the Northern region last quarter and so forth. Top-of-the-line database packages allow frequently asked questions to be pre-programmed so that they can be regularly used to compile reports by relatively unskilled keyboard operatives.

The relational database can be a very complex animal indeed and putting one together can stretch one's powers of logic to the very limit, as this writer knows to his cost. Further complications arise with the move to multi-user databases. Here the main problem is who is in control of the data, when, for example, two people want to access or update the same record at the same time. Some database programs provide an automatic record locking system, others use what is known as a 'locking strategy' which is configured by the person in charge of the database. Record security can be vitally important in database applications, especially multi-user databases containing confidential or sensitive information. All the main programs provide a variety of methods whereby records are either hidden, only inspected, reports only provided, only up-dated or full database access. This is usually achieved by a combination of differing user levels and the use of passwords.

With very large database applications even a multi-user system will be too slow and cumbersome. The usual solution is to dedicate one powerful personal computer to looking after the record tables. This is known as the database 'server' with the other users on the network being called the 'clients' hence the term 'client/server network'. In a client/server regime, the various client operations lend themselves very well to teleworking.

Leading database programs are dBase 1V and Dataease by Sapphire for DOS, while Paradox for Windows by Borland and Microsoft's Access run on the Windows platform. FileMaker Pro by Claris is a brand leader for the Apple Mac and PipeDream 3 by Colton Software is a popular package for the Acorn/Archimedes.

Finally, no treatment of databases or their uses would be complete without a reminder for any potential database user to read the requirements of the 1984 Data Protection Act.

DESKTOP PUBLISHING

The phrase 'Desktop Publishing' was first coined by the software company Aldus when it introduced its PageMaker product for the Apple Mac computer. While the gap between top flight word processing programs and DTP packages has narrowed, DTP generally has far more accurate control of typefaces and page layout as well as the overall automation of the publishing process.

As ever there is a wide variety of products available aimed at different sectors of the market. Once more it is essential to be quite clear as to what sort of output is to be produced. Is it for a newsletter, instruction manual, brochures or even books. Will it be in colour or black and white? Will it be printed in-house or through a typesetting and laser printing bureau? What sort of response time is required? A couple of thousand leaflets tomorrow poses very different problems to a system designed to produce relatively few copies of a glossy presentation document.

The nature and quality of the output is perhaps the most important consideration in DTP. The size and weight of the paper used as well as the resolution of the printing, usually measured in dots per inch (dpi) will help determine the type of printer required. A desktop laser printer may be adequate but will probably need the addition of a font manager, such as 'Postscript' by Adobe, to give the necessary variety and flexibility, an addition which can double the basic cost.

Most teleworkers in DTP are likely to be working in one discrete area of the publishing process. They may receive text electronically as a word processing file, lay it out using the DTP programme and send the completed DTP file or files to the typesetting bureau or their head office in the same way. Some workers will not need a printing capability, others will, if only to check the appearance of the printed output and perhaps also use it to supplement their teleworking income by providing a printing service to their local community.

Until recently the choice of software in the DTP arena was inextricably linked to the choice of hardware, usually the Apple Mac and UNIX Workstations. With the advent of 'Windows' with its GUI and multi-tasking features, many of the top DTP programs are now being made available for the IBM PC instead of being restricted to the Apple Mac and UNIX workstations. DTP is the one area of computing where hardware choice can override other considerations because of the domination of the Apple Mac in this sector and this very large Apple Mac installed base cannot be ignored. As always, compatibility is everything, especially for the teleworker.

Market leaders in the DTP sector are QuarkXPress and Aldus Creative 2 for the Mac, with Aldus PageMaker 4.0, Ventura Publisher 4.0 and Framemaker for Windows being the leading 'DOS with Windows' packages for the IBM PC. Genesis II is a leading DTP package for the Acorn/ Archimedes.

GRAPHICS

While the computer generated graphics sector has just under 7 per cent of the UK software market, reductions in the cost of personal computer processing power coupled with technological advances have made it very much a growth area. This sector also encompasses an ever widening area, from producing slides for a business presentation through free-hand artwork for printing and publishing to colour photograph re-touching. Like DTP, this is a sector that has been and continues to be dominated by the graphics-oriented Apple Macintosh computer but this domination is now being seriously challenged with the advent of the 'Windows' platform for the IBM PC. Volume production of the PC has meant that the cost of a 486 PC with the necessary power to handle professional colour, is now much less than an equally potent Apple Mac. It remains to be seen whether this price advantage will be enough to successfully storm the Apple-controlled bastions of desktop colour imaging.

In common with the other software sectors, Graphics packages come with a wide variety of capabilities and are priced accordingly. Once again it is vital to analyse carefully exactly what one wants to do and what market sector is being targeted. For business presentations, word charts are the main requirement coupled with some graphing capability for the numeric data. Make sure a wide range of charts is provided; bar, pie, exploded-pie together with a 3D facility. An ability to mix words and graphs on the same chart may be essential and an importing system allowing one to import text or numeric data from another application program can usefully speed up the creation process. Wide selections of 'clip art' are available and are invaluable to those not of an artistic bent. Clip art is usually loaded from a floppy disk and many add-on libraries are available to supplement that included in any particular package.

Colour imaging is at the top-end of the graphics sector and here productivity is more important than price. The crucial link in the productivity chain is the software that manipulates the image and then produces the output in the correct format. It should also be noted that packages designed to handle natural images such as photographs or video stills need special image processing tools to cope with the far subtler changes, as in a photograph, than those found in computer generated artwork created with a paint or drawing programme.

A major stumbling block to the continued expansion of desktop colour imaging is the lack of an industry-wide standard for colour calibration, vital if you are to be sure what you see on the screen is what you will see in the printed output. At present a number of vendors have introduced their own colour matching technologies with no pan-industry agreement. One VDU manufacturer, Radius, has licensed a variant of the Pantone Colour Matching System, the traditional and international system for specifying print colours, but so far this has not been taken up on a large scale. Once again, teleworkers will have to be careful to ensure their system is one hundred per cent compatible with that of their clients.

It is vital to realise that professional graphics and image processing needs serious computing power. A single image can take up to seven Megabytes of data, and colour image processing puts tremendous demands on both the processor and the internal memory resource. Such performance does not come cheap, particularly when allied to the cost of some expensive peripheral devices such as scanners and digitisers. A further consideration for the teleworker is the likely volume of data to be both transmitted and received. One seven Megabyte image will take about fifty minutes to transmit over a standard modem. This would reduce to two minutes over a high performance ISDN link.

For the Apple Mac, top-of-the-range products are Pixel Paint Professional, Adobe PhotoShop, Letraset ColorStudio and Electronic Art's Studio 32. For DOS with 'Windows' comparable products are Harvard 1.01, Corel Draw 2.0, Freelance 1.0 and Powerpoint 3.0.

COMPUTER AIDED DESIGN/MANUFACTURE (CAD/CAM)

CAD

To the layperson, computer aided design (CAD) is perhaps the most impressive demonstration of the scope and power of the personal computer. Two dimensional drawings can be squeezed or stretched, a wall taken out here, a door inserted there and finally the modified entity displayed in perspective and viewed from any desired angle- as well as being coloured and shaded according to taste.

Originally, CAD's advantage was thought to be in increasing a drawing office's productivity but this has proved to be largely illusory. Now, the advantages are seen to be in the speed of product modification and shortening the lines between drawing office and production line with consequential improvements in accuracy and quality. CAD systems can also be used to test prototype designs with particular regard to stress and strain analysis as well as to estimate the quantities of materials used. A further strength of CAD is that a library of frequently used parts or symbols can be built up, reducing much of the repetition in technical drawing. Add-on libraries of specific symbols for architecture, engineering and electronic applications are available for most CAD programmes.

In parallel with developments in the other software sectors, CAD has progressed from purely drafting programmes to sundry complementary features such as shading, colouring and even animation. As a result, some of the boundaries between CAD and graphics have become very blurred indeed.

A key factor in the realm of CAD is the need to exchange data between different systems. This can be in-company or, an increasingly likely scenario, between a manufacturer and supplier or collaborative manufacturers. Since there are many CAD systems around this has been solved by the adoption of what is known as the 'neutral format' the commonest of which is DXF (data exchange format) from Autodesk, producers of the market leading CAD program AutoCAD. Although a 'neutral' format, DXF is owned and controlled by Autodesk so there has been some reluctance to its wholesale adoption by the industry. The other widely used alternative is the Initial Graphics Exchange Specification (IGES).

In common with graphics, and for the same reason, CAD uses a great deal of processor power and until fairly recently its use was confined to a very powerful species of personal computer known as a workstation. Again, the increased power and comparatively low costs of the latest generation IBM PC and their clones have brought CAD firmly into the PC arena. CAD also requires some specialised and expensive peripherals such as digitisers and plotters and the teleworker in this field will again have to consider an ISDN line to reduce the costs of high volume electronic traffic.

Cornerstone and ArchiCAD 4.0 are the leading CAD packages for the Apple Macintosh platform. AutoCAD 11 from Autodesk is the leading brand of CAD for the PC and Autodesk also has a low-end drafting program called Autosketch which is a also available for the 'Windows' platform.

CAM

CAM, when coupled with CAD refers to computer aided manufacture which is unlikely to be applicable to teleworking and is thus outside the scope of this book. On its own CAM refers to computer aided management, the use of the computer in the management of projects. Until the introduction of Microsoft's 'Project of Windows' this was a relatively unexploited software sector with just a few players with sophisticated products aimed at the government and local authority market. Microsoft's entry to the market introduced CAM to many managers under pressure to maximise limited resources and the sales of project management software are rising fast. CAM packages vary widely in both versatility and price, and cater for the needs of the occasional user on the one hand to the professional project manager on the other. However, more than in any other areas of software, CAM is one where a hands-on test drive is absolutely essential.

Apart from Microsoft, leading vendors in this sector are Symantec, Deepak Sareen Associates and Micro Planning International.

MISCELLANIA

There are a number of other software application programs which do not conveniently fit into any of the above categories and they will be treated briefly in this section.

'Group' software, sometimes known as workgroup software is at its simplest another name for electronic mail or E-Mail, and in its more complex forms covers the area of Executive Information Systems. These programs work over networks which can be local or spread over a wide area to include teleworkers. They offer a variety of facilities such as a communal diary system, bulletin boards and conferencing, as well as E-mail. Some have comprehensive database and information retrieval options. Leading products are Lotus Notes and WordPerfect Office for the PC and Meeting Maker for the Apple Mac.

A relatively new kind of software program is the 'information manager' which endeavours to emulate some people's habit of jotting down random thoughts as they occur on to a notepad. Some regard them as invaluable others that they are more trouble than they are worth; it very much depends on the individual's style of working. 'Info Select' from First Hand Software has received much critical acclaim in this field.

Accountancy software has quite deliberately been left out of this review. Selection of accounting software, of which an excellent range is now available, is critical to any enterprise and usually needs skilled professional help not least from the enterprises' own accountants. Thus while a number of accounting and book-keeping tasks are suitable for teleworking, it was not thought appropriate to consider the pros and cons of differing accounting software packages in this book.

It should also be noted that a large number of profession-specific software packages are available. These cover doctors, dentists, farmers and various branches of retailing. Information is obtained from the trade or profession specialist press.

It must also be mentioned that there is a large area of public domain software called 'Shareware'. These are programs and utilities compiled by individual programmers and which are available free of charge or for a fairly nominal fee, usually £10. A list of public domain software can be found in the specialist computer magazines.

UTILITIES

In the formative years of the personal computer, 'Utility' programs were conceived as user-friendly tool kits to help one recover from the periodic disaster, usually resulting from over-enthusiastic file deletion or a failure to understand some of the more obscure logic of one's DOS. These tool kit programs have progressively expanded their range of facilities and now incorporate basic file editing features, databases, communication programs and personal time managers. This section also refers to one or two other useful programs which do not readily fit into any other category as well as to the shareware market.

The tool kit market for the IBM PC is shared by two protagonists, Norton Utilities from Symantec and PC Tools from Centre Point. They both cost the same, £139, at the time of writing, and have a wide range of features although neither is perfect and they each have their respective strengths and weaknesses. Choice is largely a matter of personal taste. The same two companies provide similar support for the Apple Mac with Norton Utilities for the Macintosh and MAC Tools. For the Acorn/Archimedes there is The HardDisk Companion and Toolkit Plus.

A recent and well-publicised personal computer problem has been the 'Virus'. A computer virus is a program designed to surreptitiously load itself into your computer's hard disk where it will often lie dormant for a period of time before awakening to wreak some kind of havoc, such as erasing or corrupting files.

The problem is more acute with the Apple Mac than the IBM PC or the Archimedes for the technical reason that it is easier to write virus programs for the Mac than for the others. A range of Anti-Virus programs are now available across the whole range of personal computers.

COMPUTER TRAINING

Virtually everyone will benefit from some formal training in the use of computer software. All the major software programs come complete with thick manuals, very often written in quite atrocious English. How should one begin?

First, one has to appreciate that all computer software is compiled by a special sub-species of homo sapiens called the computer programmer. Computer programmers, while having superior intellects and great powers of logic are not noted for either their literacy or what the rest of us mere mortals call common sense. Consequently, they frequently lose sight of what their programs are actually intended to do, and in compiling instruction manuals have considerable trouble calling a spade a spade, never mind by any of its commoner colloquial names. Of course I am exaggerating, but only a little, and many of you will know only too well just what I mean.

There are no hard and fast rules. The first hurdle is to install the program on to your computer. Program installation varies from the "perfectly straightforward" to the "not for the faint hearted". Usually the computer supplier will have installed the operating system and often 'Windows' if appropriate. If you are buying the application programs from the hardware supplier, ask him to install them as well. If not, read through the installation procedure thoroughly several times and then do it yourself. It will be frustrating at times, with a few aborted attempts and you may even be forced to use the telephone helpline if you get really stuck, but remember, it's an important part of getting to know your computer.

Many programs come complete with a tutorial, so start working through that. You may also find it helpful to purchase one of the many third-party software handbooks that are on the market; they are usually far easier to understand having been written from the users' standpoint rather than the programmers'.

Computer training courses come in all shapes and sizes. Some of the bigger software houses regularly run courses at centres nationwide. There are many third party companies running training courses either on their own premises or on the clients'; to find them consult the Yellow Pages. Local authorities and further education establishments also run courses for specific areas such as word processing, spreadsheets and databases, and their costs are often heavily subsidised.

Whatever type of training is selected, this writer firmly believes that to get the most out of any course, you need to get in several weeks' practice beforehand. By doing so you will absorb very much more of what can be pretty rich fare. Believe it or not, computer trainers continually report that people turn to expensive courses without ever having sat at a keyboard, never mind seen the software application program.

Finally, always remember that practice makes perfect.

8 The Hardware

INTRODUCTION

In this chapter we have to get even more technical than in the previous one. However, the writer has endeavoured to describe the fundamentals in lay terms without sacrificing accuracy and so the treatment perforce does not delve into the inner reaches of computer technology. Inevitably, a number of acronyms have to be used and their meaning is given each time they are introduced. If the reader subsequently gets lost, I apologise and respectfully refer them to the Glossary.

PCs, APPLES AND ACORNS

As has been stated earlier, there is more than one variety of personal computer, and this book deals with the three main types which will be of relevance to the teleworker, the IBM PC and its look-alikes or clones, the Apple range and the Acorn/Archimedes range which are widely used in education throughout the UK.

All personal computers have the same basic components and these are illustrated in schematic form in Figure 8.1.

The central processing unit, or microprocessor, can be described as the 'engine' of the computer and it defines the basic character of these three types of computer. Each also has its own 'architecture' which defines how the various components relate to each other. The 'buses' are the paths along which the data passes to and fro within the computer and they come in different widths, referred to by the number of 'bits' they can handle at one time. The greater the number of bits the 'wider' the bus and the quicker the data can be handled by the processor, all else being equal. All processors have

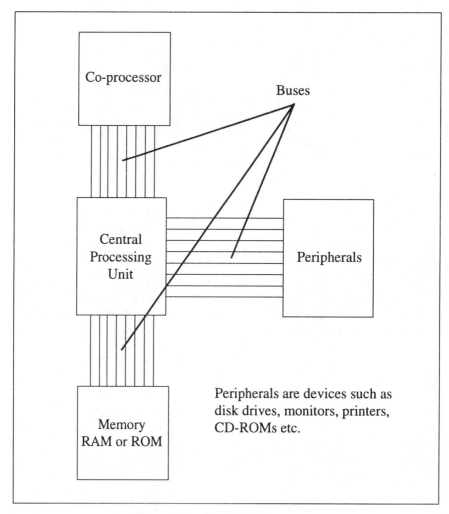

Figure 8.1   Basic Components

one or two rates at which they can operate. This is known as the 'clock speed'. A clock crystal sends pulses to the processor to synchronise its own activity with that of all the other processor chips it is connected to. Clock speeds are expressed in MHz or millions of cycles per second and vary from 4.77MHz to 50MHz for the very latest microprocessors.

To keep things fairly straightforward, each of the three main types of personal computer will be considered in turn.

THE IBM PC

The original IBM PC was introduced late in 1981. Since then the basic format has been continually developed, centred around the Intel Corporation's family of processors. The main characteristics of the various Intel processors is given in Table 1.

Table 1

Processor	Bus Int.	Ext.	Speeds, MHz	Co-Processor	MIPS
8088	8	16	5/8/10	Yes	0.20
80286	16	16	8/10/12/16	Yes	1.5
i386SX	32	16	16/20/25	Yes	5.0
i386DX	32	32	16/25/33/40	Yes	10.0
i486sx	32	32	20/25	No	10.0
i486DX	32	32	25/33/50	Built-in	27.0

The processor numbers in Table 3 refer to Intel's own nomenclature. Several other companies have managed to 'reverse engineer' Intels' processors and have produced their own versions which emulate the original in every way. The matter is now being hotly contested in the US courts.

A co-processor is a go-faster add-on chip which is essential if one is going to be using programmes which require a lot of processing power, such as graphics and DTP. When fitting a co-processor chip it is vital to ensure that its clock speed matches that of the central microprocessor.

Apart from the processor, a computer's performance depends very much on the size of its Random Access Memory, RAM. The original 8088 processor could only use 1Mb of RAM, the 20286 extended this to 4Mb and the i386 to either 16 or 32Mb while the i486 will go up to 32 or 64Mb.

All PCs will have at least one floppy disk drive and the industry is now standardising on the 3.5 inch disk which can hold 720Kb or 1.44Mb of data, although a new 2.8Mb version is in the pipeline. The larger 5.25 inch floppies with capacities of 360Kb and 1.2Mb are still in general use and it probably makes sense to have one of each. It must be clearly noted that while the high density drives of both formats can read low density disks, they cannot write to them. A low density drive will not be able to read what the high density drive has written.

The hard disk is the computer's bulk storage bin. They come in a variety of sizes, from 20Mb in steady increments up to 520Mb, all sizes coming in different diameters. While it is unlikely to interest the first-time buyer, hard disks connect to the computer in a number of different ways, called interfaces. IBM's own brand PCs, the P5/2 series use the Small Computer System Interface, SCSI. All the other PC brands will come with either an Integrated Drive Electronics, IDE, interface or the Enhanced Small Device Interface, ESDI. While the merits of these interfaces are relatively unimportant to the teleworker, it is essential to know which one your computer has so that any additional cards or devices will be compatible.

PCs also differ in what's known as their architecture or bus standards. While this makes no difference in running software, it does matter if you have to up-grade or modify the computer in any way. IBM's own brand PS/2 series have the idiosyncratic Micro Channel Architecture, MCA, bus. All other brands will have either Industry Standard Architecture, ISA, or Enhanced Standard Industry Architecture, EISA. Once again, it matters only to know what you have.

PCs are contained in a wide variety of cases, from diminutive desktops to floor standing 'tower' units. Choice is largely a matter of taste and the need for expansion in the shape of different plug-in cards. All PC specifications will state the number and type of free slots they have. Mini-tower cases are becoming popular, being a cut-down tower designed to sit on the desk beside a monitor and with plenty of scope for expansion.

An entry level PC with more than adequate performance for word processing and spreadsheets would be a 386SX running at 20MHz with 1Mb RAM and a 40Mb hard disk. 'Windows' applications really need a 386DX running at 25MHz with 4Mb RAM and 100Mb hard disk. CAD, graphics and DTP applications should have a 486DX running at 33MHz with at least 8Mb of RAM and a 210Mb hard disk to do the software justice.

THE APPLE MACINTOSH RANGE

There is only one Apple and although the range is extensive, it can only be purchased from an accredited Apple dealer. The salient features of the Apple Macintosh range are shown in Table 2.

The Classics have an integral 9 inch monochrome monitor and are suitable for word processing and spreadsheets. The Macintosh LC is the entry level colour model while the IIsi is the midrange computer. DTP and graphics professionals are more than catered for by the two Quadra machines.

It should be noted that there are a number of specialist accelerator cards from third party manufacturers available to a number of Apple Macs to compensate for the lack of co-processors.

ACORN AND ARCHIMEDES COMPUTERS.

The fortunes of Acorn Computers Ltd have been inextricably linked to the BBC micro for schools. Its Archimedes range introduced in 1987 was the first personal computer to incorporate a Reduced Instruction Set Computing, RISC, microprocessor. The Archimedes was (and is) an exceptionally fast computer and has now been superceded by a new range, and the Archimedes name has been dropped. The main feature of these new Acorn computers is given in Table 3.

The selection of an Acorn computer will probably depend on the user/client compatibility.

THE MONITOR OR VISUAL DISPLAY UNIT

The monitor or Visual Display Unit (VDU), is the visual interface between

Model	Processor	Co-processor	RAM	Colour	Sound
Colour Classic	16MHz 68030	Yes	4–10	Yes	Yes
Mac LC II	16MHz 68030	No	4–10	Optional	Yes
Mac LC III	25MHz 68030	Yes	4–36	Optional	Yes
Mac IIvx	32MHz 68030	Yes	4–68	Optional	Yes
Centris 610	20MHz 68040	No	4–68	Optional	Yes
Centris 650	25MHz 68040	Yes	4–132	Yes	Yes
Quadra 800	33MHz 68040	Built in	16–256	Yes	Yes
Quadra 950	40MHz 68040	Built in	16–256	Yes	Yes

Table 2   Apple Macintosh Range

Table 3   Acorn Computers (features)

Model	Processor	RAM	Hard Disk, Mb
A3020	ARM250	2–4	60
A4000	ARM250	2–4	80
A5000	ARM3	2–4	80–120
A540	ARM3	4–16	120

you and your computer; irrespective of the hardware or the software, the monitor is where the action appears to be. Since most personal computers have been sold complete with a monitor, monitors tend to have been taken for granted, and only in specialist applications such as CAD or DTP was the quality of the screen image a major consideration.

The arrival in the IBM PC domain of 'MS Windows' and its graphical user interfaces (GUIs) is one of the reasons that has led to the basic characteristics of the monitor being subjected to much closer scrutiny. The other one is a much more emotive subject; does the radiation from the monitor represent a health hazard. As yet there is no proven link between VDU use and problems in pregnancy, but several new international standards have been introduced restricting emissions even further. That alone will be enough to persuade many people to consider an alternative monitor to the one supplied as standard with their computer.   What appears on the screen of a monitor inextricably depends on the nature of the signal coming from the computer which is in turn controlled by the graphics card. What appears on the screen is limited by the output of the graphics card, and if the two are not compatible then the theoretical benefits of a new high performance monitor will remain just that, theoretical.

A number of factors govern the nature of the image on the monitor's screen. A pixel is one of the tiny dots on the screen that collectively make up the picture, and the number of pixels displayed on the screen, 640 x 480 for example, gives its resolution. The more pixels displayed, the higher the resolution. There are a number of standards of video displays in use and these are briefly described as follows:

- VGA, Video Graphics Array, current standard set by IBM, 640 x 480 pixels and 16 colours.

- Super VGA, a standard created by third party card manufacturers, 800 x 600 pixels and 256 colours.

- 8514/A, an IBM extension of VGA which "sort of" matches Super VGA using a technique called interlacing.

- XGA, Extended Graphics Array, being promoted by IBM as the future industry standard, 1,024 x 768 pixels and 256 colours

Cursory examination of the above standards indicates some duplication, but, without getting over technical, that is not in fact the case and although Super VGA and 8514/A can produce displays of similar quality, it is done in a different way and different software is required.

The other factors which govern image quality are the 'dot pitch', the 'refresh rate' and the type of screen mask that is used. Dot pitch refers simply to the size of the pixels, the common one being 0.31mm. Other pitches are 0.28 and 0.26mm; as a general guide, the smaller the pitch the crisper the image. The refresh rate is the speed at which the beam of electrons sweeps along the lines of pixels illuminating them. The standard IBM PC has a screen refresh rate of around 50Hz, the same as a television set, in Apple Macs it is 60.15Hz. High performance monitors have a refresh rate of around 72Hz and because we humans have what is known as 'persistance of vision' these higher refresh rates make a tremendous difference to viewing quality, the screen image appearing much more solid with a complete absence of flickering.

As with television sets, the cathode ray tube in monitors come in two main varieties, the three gun tube and the Sony 'Trinitron'. Unlike the TV market, the difference in the two types at the higher resolutions used in high performance monitors, is much more marked than with a TV picture, with Sony's 'Trinitron' having a considerable advantage (usual disclaimer).

Unlike the TV market, 'Trinitron' screens are to be found in monitors produced by a number of big-name manufacturers other than Sony. All sale brochures will clearly state the dot pitch, the refresh rate or rates and the type of screen being used.

While the price of a standard 14 inch monitor equates to that of a 14 inch colour TV set, around £250, for reasons best known to the manufacturers, prices for large screen monitors rapidly take off into the stratosphere. Monitors of 16 and 17 inch range from £900 to £1,500 while 20 and 21 inch monitors go from £1,500 to £2,500. Certainly it will pay to shop around, these are list prices and on the street prices can be a bit lower. However, for the moment at least, large screen computer monitors cost serious money and you must remember that you may also need a new graphics card.

The ability of a graphics card depends on its own processor and its amount of memory. As ever, performance equates to price; a basic VGA card with 256Kb of memory costs about £40 while an advanced card for CAD applications with a potent processor and 1Mb of memory can cost up to £1,000. Unless you are very confident, never buy a monitor without seeing it working with the software you will be using and the same graphics card you have or intend to buy. It is also vital to ensure that your software can recognise the high resolutions large monitors can offer, or that a monitor bought for, say, DTP can adjust to a lower resolution to accommodate a word processing or database application.

Although evidence on the danger to health from prolonged exposure to the radiation from computer monitors is inconclusive, there is no doubt that all monitors do emit several kinds of radiation. The debate, if that is the right word, is about what are the safe levels for each type of radiation. Sweden has been the leading country in establishing standards, the latest of which is the oft-quoted MPR2 which was issued in 1990. Britain expects to issue a Health and Safety (Display Screen Equipment) Regulation in 1993, and of course there is the EEC Directive 90/270 covering all the working conditions pertaining to the office which comes into force in January 1993. For those with any concerns in this matter, you should ensure that a monitor meets the Swedish MPR2 standard and is not just marked as being 'low radiation'. Expect to pay a premium of £70–£100 for this extra protection.

A word of warning here for Apple Mac users. Unlike the IBM PC, the Macintosh sensibly relates the resolution to the size of the monitor screen and a special sensing line tells the Mac what size of monitor it is connected to and thus what screen resolution to send to it. Some Apples only work at a resolution 640 x 480 pixels, others, notably the Quadra range, recognise 640 x 480, 832 x 624 and 1152 x 870 resolutions. Be absolutely sure the monitor you select is fully compatible and is supplied with the correct cabling.

Perhaps the best advice in selecting a monitor is to ignore all the technical mumbo jumbo and simply rely on your own eyes; if it looks good it probably is good. Do give a monitor a fairly realistic trial; after all, you are going to be sitting in front of it for long periods. Remember also that a large monitor takes up a great deal of desk space, not just for itself, but because you will also have to sit further away from it to maximise its benefits and avoid eye strain.

KEYBOARDS AND MICE

While all personal computers are supplied with a keyboard, an increasing number of third party manufacturers are offering keyboards with a superior design or feel and also with a variety of special features.

Keyboards have one of two main types of key layout, the 84 key AT type with 10 function keys at the left hand side of the keyboard and the 101 key Enhanced type with the function and four other keys along the top of the keyboard. The AT type is a bit old hat now and virtually all computers are supplied with a 101 key enhanced keyboard.

Keyboards differ in detailed design, some having flat keyboard surfaces, others being slightly concave. The 'feel' of the keys is important but very much a matter of personal taste; some people like a definite mechanical click, others a softer, quieter feel to the keys.

Some specialist keyboards which incorporate one or two sets of extra function keys are available. This enables one to have a set of function keys for a specific programme. Software manufacturers frequently supply keyboard templates to remind the user what functions each key has for that application, and these are designed to fit over or above the function keys in each type of keyboard. With these special keyboards, the left hand set of function keys can be set for, say Word Perfect, with the top set for Lotus 123. Other variations incorporate a 'trackerball' in the keyboard itself to save having a separate mouse or trackerball on the desk.

Keyboards have two particular allergies; they do not like coming into contact with beverages of any kind nor to they react kindly to be clogged up with cigarette ash. Keyboards do appreciate being kept clean and are usually provided with a clear acrylic protective cover for when they are not being used. Soft, clear protective membranes are now available which allow protected use of the keyboard while sacrificing some feel, for the benefit of tea swilling, chain smoking teleworkers.

In computing parlance, a mouse is a device which converts motion on the desktop to motion of an arrow, usually called a cursor on the monitor screen. They function in one of two ways. The most common form is the opto-mechanical mouse which uses a rolling ball in the base of the mouse to sense the direction and velocity of any movement and convert it to an electrical signal. A 'trackerball' is an upside down opto-mechanical mouse where the fingers or thumb give the ball its motion instead of moving a mouse all over a desk. Optical mice use an infra-red beam bounced off a special reflective mat to sense any movement. They have the advantage of having no moving parts and are very sensitive but do of course have to be used on the special pad or mat supplied with them.

Mice are connected to the computer in a number of ways, depending on the computer. Apple, Acorn/Archimedes, IBM PS series, Compaq and an increasing number of PC look-alikes are fitted with a dedicated mouse port. For other PCs, mice either plug into a free serial port (a serial mouse) or into a special card that has to be fitted in one of the expansion slots in the computer (a bus mouse). All mice need special software, called 'mouse drivers' to be installed before they will work. Nowadays, most computers can be supplied with a mouse and the software already installed.

Opto-mechanical mice function best on a mouse mat which is about 9 inches square and has a textured surface to stop the ball slipping and sliding about, something that happens all too readily on a shiny desktop. Mouse mats also help to keep the ball clean and free from extraneous material which can adversely affect the rodents' performance.

As indicated above, trackerballs are upside down mice operated by the fingers and thus do not have to be moved around. A number of specialised trackerballs are now available for attachment to notebook sized portable computers to give them a mouse capability. There are also one or two more novel pointing devices, notably the 'mousepen' which, as its name suggests, is the outcome of an unlikely union between a opto-mechanical mouse and a ball-point pen.

PRINTERS

Some teleworkers may feel a printer is an unnecessary expense as all their output is going to be electronically transmitted; others will need hard copy to assess progress or the quality of their chosen work. Given the wide choice of printers now available coupled with continuously falling prices, it seems unduly parsimonious not to have some kind of printing capability with every personal computer.

In choosing a printer one must first consider the application programmes being used and what range of printer emulations they support. Printer emulations are sets of instructions which a programme sends via the computer to the printer and tell it how to produce its output. All printers will support at least one emulation, and all application programmes support a number of printers through a number of sub-programmes called printer drivers. Thus to ensure the best performance from a printer, you must ensure that its emulations match those of the application programmes you have selected.

Having established which emulations the printer must have, it remains to decide about the other main requirements of a printer; the quality of the printed output and its paper handling ability. With regard to the quality of printed output, there are three main types of printer, the dot-matrix or pin printer, the ink-jet or bubble-jet printer and the laser printer. Each type has its pros and cons and comes with a wide range of facilities and prices. The daisy wheel printer, familiar to those of you who have an Amstrad PCW is now obsolete.

In a dot-matrix printer the print-head has a number of pins, 9, 18, 24, and rarely, 48, which in the right combination strike the paper through an inked ribbon so forming the characters. The larger the number of pins in the print-head, the better the quality of the print. Dot-matrix printers usually run in two different modes, draft mode and Near Letter Quality (NLQ) mode, NLQ mode being very much slower than draft mode. Dot-matrix printers have two major disadvantages, they are slow (note that their speed is always expressed in characters per second, cps, not in pages per minute) and they are very noisy. Their advantages are that they are the only printers that can handle continuous stationery by means of a tractor feed and in 80 or 132 column widths, and they are the cheapest printers available, with prices starting at £150 for a 9 pin and £200 for a 24 pin model in 80 column form. It should be noted here that the cost in many of the expensive dot-matrix printers is for their heavy duty build quality which is essential in a busy office environment but which would be wasted on the average teleworker.

Ink-jet printers are having a resurgence in popularity due in no small measure to the introduction of small, portable inkjet printers from Canon and Kodak. Ink-jet printers work by directing fine sprays of ink on to the paper from multiple nozzles on an ink cartridge which moves to and fro across the paper. The quality of output is quite outstanding and ink-jet printers are now considered "the poor man's laser". The advantages of the ink-jet are its quietness and its print quality with regard to its cost. The disadvantages are slowness, one A4 typed page in about 70 seconds, and limited paper handling ability. Portable ink-jet printers can only handle one sheet of paper at a time unless one buys a cut sheet feeder which can hold up to 50 sheets and costs around £50. Portable ink-jets cost from about £250, while desktop ink-jets are from £300 upwards. Only a few desktop ink-jet printers can handle continuous stationery but most have provision for two separate cut sheet feeders although a second one can be quite an expensive extra. Ink-jet printing also offers the lowest cost entry to colour printers with the Hewlett Packard PaintJet at around £600.

A few words of caution regarding ink-jet printers. Firstly, ink-jet printer emulations are not very widely supported by software, so remember to check compatibility with your software. Secondly, one should always remember that the ink is water soluble and will become illegible if rained on or otherwise wetted.

Although prices have come down dramatically over the past few years, laser printers are still expensive by most people's standards with the cheapest now costing around £700. They do however offer quite outstanding print quality, often indistinguishable from typeset work. The main factors affecting the performance and cost of a laser printer are its range of typefaces or fonts as they are more correctly known, the size of its memory and its printing speed.

The wide range and size of fonts that can be reproduced by a laser printer is controlled by what is called a 'page description language'. PostScript by Adobe is the original and most widely used page description language and laser printers which recognise this language are usually described as a 'PostScript' printer. This capability, which does allow access to an enormous range of fonts and scaleable typefaces does not come cheap and a 'PostScript' printer will be typically £600 more than its non-PostScript equivalent. Hewlett-Packard who have probably done more than anyone to foster the widespread adoption of the laser printer have now produced their own PCL5 language, but this recent development may be overtaken by 'TrueImage' a new page description language being developed by Microsoft in association with Apple Computer Inc. For the teleworker who is specialising in DTP or graphics, a PostScript capability will be mandatory, while H-P PCL5 or the Laserjet 2 or 3 emulations will be sufficient for the rest of us mortals. It should also be noted that many laser printers can accept font cartridges from third party suppliers such as 'Bitstream' which can considerably increase their flexibility. Once more, be sure to check that the printer can be driven by your software.

A basic laser printer has a printing speed of four pages per minute which should be more than adequate for personal use. What can be more important in governing printing speed is how much of the information about the document to be printed can be stored by the printer while it translates it into printing commands. For this reason, laser printers are always quoted as having so much memory. For only typewritten material, 512Kb is sufficient but anyone contemplating any kind of DTP or graphics should insist on a minimum of 2Mb.

All laser printers handle cut sheet paper in A4 and other business sizes. Many can be fitted with double sheet feeders, one for plain and one for headed paper although once again, extra paper bins or cassettes can be expensive.

While the running costs of a printer are unlikely to be a crucial factor in the selection process, they should be borne in mind if only because of the differing amounts involved. A ribbon for a dot-matrix printer costs about £5 and will last for around 300 A4 typed pages. An ink-jet cartridge costs £14 and will also last for 300 pages. A replacement toner cartridge for a laser printer will cost £50 and last for about 4,500 pages but the laser printer will also need its drum replaced after 25,000 pages and its fuser after 50,000 pages and these can cost £130 and £70 respectively. If buying a laser printer the supplier should be able to give you an accurate estimate of its running costs.

Summarising, dot-matrix printers are cheap, cheerful and noisy, lasers fabulous but expensive while ink-jets lie somewhere in between. A good middle-of-the-road choice, and that of the writer, is a portable ink-jet with a cut sheet feeder which combines good quality output with reasonable cost with the added bonus that it is ideal for taking on business trips to accompany a notebook computer.

PLOTTERS

Plotters are the output devices which produce a drawing or diagram on paper from the computer derived data of a CAD programme. Full size plotters for A0 or A1 paper are large and expensive pieces of kit whose use is restricted to the professional drawing office. Nevertheless, CAD does lend itself to teleworking and a number of smaller and affordable plotters are available for the teleworking CAD specialists who need to produce their own hard copy.

At this 'entry level' as it were, plotters will be one of two types, ink-jet or pen. The ink-jet technology is identical to that used in the printers described above. It should be noted here that both ink-jet and laser printers do have a 'plotting' capability but are restricted to monochrome and in the size of paper they can handle, usually A4 and foolscap. Hewlett-Packard is the leading manufacturer of small ink-jet plotters with its range of 'Graphics' and 'Graphics Plus' machines which can handle upto six colours on A3 paper. Prices range from £1,000 to £2,500,

Pen plotters use one or more pens which create the drawing by being moved over the paper by a carriage which can move along both the horizontal and vertical axes. Roland are the leading brand with pen plotters for both A4 and A3 paper with a range of facilities. Costs vary from £450 to £1,000.

Ink-jet plotters are faster than pen plotters, but neither is a match for the speed of a full sized professional electrostatic thermal plotter, a difference that is reflected in the price of these machines.

Computer Aided Design professionals will need no reminding that it is essential that one selects a plotter that is fully compatible with the command language of the software being used.

SCANNERS

A scanner enables one to transfer images or text straight from the page into a computer where, using appropriate software, it can be converted into a form the computer can use. Scanners have three main uses. They are used to scan graphics and photographs so that they can be incorporated in a document. They can also be used, with the aid of special software, to transfer text directly into the computer without having to key it in via the keyboard. This feature is known as Optical Character Recognition, OCR. Lastly, they are used in Document Image Processing, DIP, where the documents are stored as images instead of as text files.

Since scanners are expensive, one has to make sure that the advantages they offer outweigh the costs. One also has to make sure that the scanner is suited to its intended purpose, a scanner that is superb at transferring colour photographs may be poor at OCR or not even have an OCR capability. It is also essential to appreciate that a scanner's performance is largely dependent on the accompanying software. Thus a scanner must not be assessed in isolation but in conjunction with scanning software and most suppliers sell scanners bundled with a suitable software package.

There are three main categories of scanner available, handheld, flatbed and roll-feed. Hand-held scanners are exactly that, and you slowly and steadily pull them across the paper or photo you wish to be scanned. They have a restricted scanning width of about four inches and the quality of the output depends to a large extent on the skill of the user.

Flatbed scanners are the mainstream scanners for the business market. They work rather like a photocopier with the paper containing the text or image to be scanned placed on a glass plate and secured beneath a hinged lid. Some flatbed scanners have optional automatic sheet feeders for large volume work. Roll-feed scanners are rather like fax machines in that the sheet of paper to be scanned is fed into the scanner and is scanned as it passes over a drum.

Depending on their use, scanners have to cope with some conflicting requirements and as always the outcome is a compromise. Image recognition requires the ability to detect a range of 'greyscales', a number of shades of grey from pure white to jet black. For image transfer 64 is the minimum acceptable and for really high quality transfer one should have 256. On the other hand, for OCR the scanner needs only to be able to detect text which is either black or white. The ability to handle colour may be more important than you think; what colour is the text you wish to scan, are you sure it is all in black and not in green, blue or brown? Most of us have seen the peculiar effects when one photocopies a document with text or images in different colours; some colours are ignored by the monochrome process. It should also be noted that even the best OCR programmes are not 100% accurate; 98% is about the best that can be achieved, so scanned material should always be checked for accuracy and errors corrected.

Two other factors also have to be considered when choosing a scanner; the resolution of the scanner and the file compatibility of the software. For OCR, a resolution of 300 dpi, the same as a laser printer will be adequate but for very high quality image transfer you will have to look for something with a resolution approaching 1,200 dpi. Regarding file output, there is little point in having a scanner if its output cannot be used by your other software. OCR software should be able to output in ASCII, Microsoft Word, WordPerfect and WordStar formats. For graphics, PXC and TIFF are the most widely used file formats.

Finally there is the small matter of hooking the scanner up to your computer. All scanners need an adapter card which fits in to one of the expansion slots in the computer. Ideally one should use an SCSI card which permits very high data transfer rates, but be absolutely sure it is compatible with your computer's architecture. With regard to prices, small hand scanners start at about £275, flat-beds at £650 and colour at around £1,600.

BACK-UP DEVICES

Backing up the information in a computer is something every computer user is continually exhorted to do and is something that is almost always ignored. Some users, of whom the writer is one, use the hard disk only for application programmes and all files are kept on floppy disks which can then be periodically copied.

Others laboriously copy the contents of their hard disk onto a series of floppies. The best and most professional approach is to use a device specifically for backing up your data, the commonest of which is a tape streamer.

A tape streamer uses magnetic tape in a cassette to digitally record all the information held on a computer's hard disk. They can be fitted internal or external and come with different capacities and transfer speeds. Connection to the computer is via the parallel port or an adapter card. Storage capacities vary according to the type of cassette used and whether the streamer uses some form of data compression. The cheapest internal streamers cost £220 and external models start at £300.

A new technique called rewritable optical disk technology is beginning to be used for back-up purposes. At present it is very expensive and its use limited to large enterprises with substantial volumes of data. There is no doubt that within a few years it will become much more affordable, by which time it can be considered a realistic alternative for the teleworker.

In concluding this section, it cannot be over-emphasised how important it is to store back-up data, in whatever shape or form, well away from the computer. If there is more than one copy, then one must be kept at a separate location, a bank safe deposit box if necessary. Remember, fires do occasionally happen, and rather more often than we think.

CD-ROM

The Compact Disc - Read Only Memory is a fairly new storage medium for the personal computer but one that has tremendous potential. Its attraction is that the CD can hold a vast amount of textual information, about 250,000 typed A4 pages, and these pages can be recalled and read using the computer. Up until now utilisation of the CD-ROM has been fairly slow due to the CD-ROM drive units being expensive and the software being rather limited (and expensive) with a strong North American bias.

The situation is now improving rapidly with internal CD-ROM drives now available for around £400, external ones for £500 and these usually come bundled with some disks. Some 2,000 titles are now available varying from the Guinness Book of Records through a variety of technical and information databases to the Official Airlines Guide which is updated every quarter. The more sophisticated disks combine illustrations and graphics with text and future developments will include sound as well (see Multimedia).

CD-ROMs are connected to the computer via an adapter card which again will have to match the computer's architecture. The CD-ROM comes with a software pack and is configured as another hard drive, although obviously it can only be read from and not written to.

MULTIMEDIA

According to its supporters and not a few vested interests, Multimedia is expected to be the growth area in personal computing during the next few years. At its simplest, multimedia adds two new types of data, sound and vision to that which can be handled already by the computer. As yet there is no one single type of multimedia application although as the concept is established a number of categories will no doubt emerge. One likely area will be a variant of the CD-ROM which will have text, sound, still pictures and video clips all combined, tailored for both recreational and educational purposes.

The Apple Macintosh range of computers has long had a sound capability but until recently the PC has been limited to emitting only bleeps from its built-in loudspeaker.

The multimedia sector has developed its own standard called Media Control Architecture, MCA, and which must not to be confused with another MCA, IBM's Micro Channel Architecture. This sets uniform standards for multimedia add-ons such as CD-ROMs, sound cards and video cards. A number of computer manufacturers are now producing Multimedia PCs with the sound and vision cards already fitted while a number of packaged multimedia kits are available to convert existing PCs, although it should be noted that these are primarily aimed at the domestic market.

There have been two main challenges in the development of multimedia for the PC. The first has been the need to integrate two new types of file, sound and vision into the computer in a form that the computer and its existing software can recognise and handle. The second has been that these two forms of media, when converted to a digital format, take up a great deal of space. A single picture frame can take 0.75Mb so one second of video can take up to 19Mb while one second of sound takes about 44Kb. The first has been largely solved by using 'MS Windows' with its capability for creating new applications. One of 'MS Windows' attributes is that it defines its main file types itself. This means that any software created by other software houses to run on the 'Windows' platform can share data and work together without any compatibility problems. Microsoft is currently working on a system in which one will be able to annotate a cell in its Excel spreadsheet with a verbal comment such as "We must try and reduce these overheads, George".

Getting the sound and vision into the computer is rather more complicated.

Sound cards can convert incoming sound from a microphone or other input into digital signals and back again. They normally have an amplifier to drive a pair of loudspeakers and a socket for connection to an electronic keyboard or sound synthesiser, called a Musical Instrument Digital Interface, MIDI, socket. The market leader and standard setter for soundcards is Creative Labs. whose 'Soundblaster' card costs £150.

Image capture is even more complex. Still images can be collected with a scanner, but live video sequences are a different matter. Technology cannot yet cope with compressing and processing 25 full frames a second. The best standard currently available is Desktop Digital Video Interactive, DVI which is still very limited in terms of quality. Video cards are still expensive and limited in capability and perhaps their greatest use at present is in the fields of animation and film and video titling. Market leaders for video cards are Videologic IBM and Intel.

As one might expect, the large amounts of data used in multimedia require considerable number crunching power and the choice of computer has to be made accordingly. Domestic multimedia can be obtained at a reasonable cost but at present professional systems stretch the power of the personal computer to its very limits and are correspondingly expensive.

The compilation of multimedia output is most simply achieved by way of a software application programme known as an 'authoring tool'. Examples of these are 'Multimedia Toolbook' by Asymetrix for 'Windows' and 'MacroMind Director 3.0' by Computers Unlimited for the Apple Mac.

9   Putting it all Together

THE BUSINESS PLAN

Business Plans are drawn up for one of two purposes. The usual one is to formalise a proposal to borrow funds, either from a bank or a venture capitalist but it should be noted they are invariably required to support any form of grant application. The other main purpose is to provide a business or enterprise with a set of goals or objectives and the strategy by which these objectives will be achieved. The objective of the business plan will influence the plan's style and content.

The individual wishing to join the teleworking fraternity may think that drawing up a business plan for a one man or women business is, as they say, a bit over the top. On the contrary, it should be seen as being a vital component of that first crucial step in making a successful and permanent entrance into the teleworking field. The essential components of an effective business plan must deal with, in order of importance, the market and marketing, the product and production, and lastly the financial aspects. These elements are as relevant to the service sector, such as teleworking, as they are to the manufacturing sector. One must always remember that fundamental maxim of business: no customers, no business.

This section will concentrate on how to produce an effective business plan to obtain a loan in order to start operating as a teleworker.

To produce an effective and persuasive business plan a considerable amount of work has to be done before pen is ever put to paper. We shall assume at this stage that at least some homework has been done; the family are going to be supportive, you have got or have acquired the right skills, and you have identified but probably not yet contacted some potential clients. It is at this stage that the impoverished prospective teleworker meets Catch 22.

It is a cardinal rule of selling that the salesperson has to be able to deliver the goods or service pretty damn quickly. When a customer has made a buying decision he or she wants to see the product or service within the week if not the next day. They do not take kindly, having made a decision, to being told that they are going to have to wait a couple of months before they can have what they've just ordered. Prospective teleworkers who do not already have the hardware and software all set up and raring to go know that with the best will in the world it will be several weeks if not a couple of months before they can start offering a service.

If you are in this situation, the solution is to make it perfectly clear at your initial contact meeting with a prospective client, that you are not selling anything but are conducting a marketing study into teleworking. Is the contact familiar with teleworking? Do they appreciate the benefits that teleworking could bring to their company? In this way the prospect does not get overly excited only to be let down on discovering that the service is not immediately available. Do not at this first meeting, unless specifically asked, indicate that you yourself intend to be a teleworker. Such an approach also conveys to the prospect that you are treating the concept in a thoroughly professional manner.

Contacting prospective companies needs some preparation in order to be successful. Obviously the very nature of a business's operations will make it more or less receptive to the concept of teleworking. Above all, make sure you are talking to the right person, the decision maker. There is nothing worse than having spent an hour putting forward a persuasive case only to be told by the prospect that he will have to discuss it with his boss.

If you have progressed to the stage of actually selling a teleworking service, do remember the points made at the conclusion of Chapter 7. To recap, always emphasise the benefits and advantages of the service to a prospective client. Demonstrate how the client will save money, provide a better service, have better information or whatever, but do not go on about how you need the work, or that teleworking is the breakthrough you've been looking for. Businessmen generally are a pretty hard-nosed bunch, and are loathe to spend anything unless there is a financial gain from doing so or a financial penalty if they don't. When planning your pitch, and plan it you must, always try to put yourself, mentally at least, in the other fellow's shoes.

It is also important at this stage to have formed a realistic idea of what your charges will be. There is little point in extolling the features of your service if the price is pitched far too high. Find out who the competition is. Is there anyone else trying to do the same as you? If there is, you will have to find something that will give your service that little extra, a competitive edge, over your rivals. Be quicker, smarter, better, cheaper or just more flexible. It is not enough just to be different. Are you in fact going to be competing with the organisation's own typing pool or will you be trying to provide an extra dimension to the organisation's present services? Perhaps you have read that the company has won a new contract order and are going to have to embark on an expensive expansion programme. These suggestions should give you some idea how to structure your own approach and to maximise its impact.

No-one is likely to come away from a series of initial client meetings with a sheaf of signed contracts or declarations clutched in their hot sticky hand. However, the findings of these preliminary meetings should give you a good feel for the nature of the marketplace. Contacts can be graded into probables, possibles and doubtfuls. It is a good idea at this stage to do some costings to find out how much work you will need to break even. These costs should take into account all your incidental costs as well as your fee income and do allow a realistic level of personal drawings. Potential lenders are as wary of people who think they can live off unrealistically low earnings as they are of those who propose excessive salaries.

The prospective teleworker should now be in a position to start fleshing out the marketing component of the business plan. It should clearly refer to the results of the market study and any statements made qualified and supported, if appropriate by statistics. All sources of any information used must also be quoted. It has to be realised that your own enthusiasm for teleworking is unlikely to be shared by others, and all the claims made in the marketing statement should be tempered with caution. Any prospective lender has to be convinced that your business plan is realistic and credible.

In format, the business plan should have a brief introduction which highlights the main purpose of the plan, for example, to borrow £2,500 over a period of two years in order to be a teleworking secretary. There then should be a brief description of the applicant, with emphasis on the appropriate skills. The vital marketing study comes next, how and where the work will come from. Usually details about manufacturing or production would come next in a prototypical business plan. In the teleworker's case this will be a detailed description of all the hardware and software needed to set up the service, together with all the costs. It must also include reference to the provision of workspace and, if appropriate, details of how any social problems, such as pre-school children will be dealt with. Do not forget to include the cost of a dedicated phone line if you think it necessary.

We now come to the financial section of the business plan. Many see this as the most important part of the business plan and there is no doubt that the financial projections have to stack up. However, in the light of some recent financial catastrophes of considerable magnitude, lenders are paying very much more attention to the narrative of the business plan rather than to the reams of immaculately presented financial projections.

While the personal computer and the spreadsheet has made relatively easy to produce extremely detailed financial projections and sensitivity analyses, one must remember that they are only projections. All the data they contain is based on someone's judgement, opinion or sometimes just a plain guess, as to what any of a number of conditions might be sometime in the future. Does anyone know what the bank rate or the dollar-sterling exchange rate will be a year hence? On what basis, in a recession, can anyone say a new product will achieve a market penetration of 15 percent within a year. The validity of these judgements depends entirely on the credibility of the person or persons making them. Thus the successful business plan has to explain in some detail, through personal history or track record, market research and anything else that can be brought to bear, why these assessments are to be believed. It also makes good sense to use one of the most powerful capabilities of the spreadsheet to provide a number of "what if?" scenarios. What if the bank rate goes up 5%? What will happen if revenues fall by 10% or overheads rise by 10%? Inclusion of such sensitivity analyses shows a prospective lender that you are realistic and not looking out on the world through rose-tinted glasses.

Any business depends on two sorts of funds. One is the capital used to buy assets, sometimes called fixed capital, the other is the cash used in the day to day running of the business, and is called the working capital. Business performance is largely assessed on two key financial documents, the profit & loss account and the balance sheet.

The profit & loss account, as its name suggests, indicates whether the trading activities of the company are making money, i.e. profitable or are losing money. A business plan must have a projected profit and loss account, expressed on a monthly basis for the first two years of activity. Accurate business projections for more than two years hence are, in the author's opinion, verging on the realms of fantasy. As well as all the revenues it must show all the expenditure the business will incur, including professional fees, bank charges and any interest and loan repayments. Many banks and training and enterprise companies provide pro-forma business plans. These will have a profit & loss account template containing the headings for all the normal items of expenditure. If you are going to use one of these prepared forms, make some photocopies of it first to check out the numbers before making a fair copy for submission.

The purpose of the balance sheet is to show the source of the funds used in a business and how they were used; their application. Balance sheets can be very confusing to the uninitiated and it is important to appreciate that the situation depicted in a balance sheet is a 'snapshot' of the state of affairs at one specific moment in time. Thus examination of one balance sheet on its own is not very informative, one has to see prior ones as well in order to see the trends. The drawing up of a balance sheet, if required, is best left to one's accountant.

For a sole trader such as the teleworker, it is vital to understand the need for some ready cash, usually referred to as "working capital" in running any business. Most businesses operate on credit and when you starts work as a teleworker you will probably not be able to issue your first invoice until the end of the first month. That invoice may not be paid for six to eight weeks, so one is effectively working for nothing for the first three months. After that, hopefully, you will receive monthly payments on a regular basis, but the business plan has to show how one is going to manage for that initial three month period and beyond, as the initial debt is unlikely to be wiped out by that first payment. The movement of cash in and out of a business is shown in the cash flow statement. This is concerned solely with the monthly movement of cash in and out of the business. The cash flow statement is connected to the profit & loss account in that each cost or revenue will be found on both but will occur at different times.

For example, a sale of £1,500 in month 1 could well appear as cash inflow in month 3. Some cash outflows will be weekly or monthly, others such as telephone charges will be quarterly. These different timings impact crucially on one's cash requirements and a cash flow statement can show that while a new business is trading profitably at its predicted level, it may not become completely cash positive for nine months to a year from start-up. A cash-flow statement for the first two years is absolutely mandatory in every business plan.

If one is not using a pro-forma business plan, do take time to lay out and present the plan in a professional manner. Given that one is proposing to be a teleworker, it really has to be done on a personal computer with a word processing programme and a spreadsheet facility. You may have to beg or scrounge access to one, but remember the presentational quality of the business plan will say a great deal about your own computer skills. If in doubt, get some help.

Once the business plan is accepted, it does not get thrown to one side and forgotten about. The fledgling business should be constantly referring to the plan to see how the predicted figures compare with what is actually achieved. Any budget projection, be it profit & loss or cash flow, is a complete waste of time and paper if it is not continually compared with the real numbers as they occur, and corrective measures taken as required. As has been stated before, lenders start getting uncomfortable when they feel borrowers are not in full control of their businesses. Business plans are not engraved on tablets of stone. They must be changed as circumstances change but of course one has to keep one's lenders fully aware of these changes and why they are necessary. This should not present a problem, on the contrary it should demonstrate to them that you are in full command of your business.

LOANS AND GRANTS

A loan is a loan and has to be paid back in full at some time in the future. They can be interest-free, at a fixed rate of interest, or subject to the vagaries of bank base rate. All prospective borrowers should fully understand all the implications of a loan and be able to show how the interest will be paid during the period as well as how the loan itself will be paid back at the end of the allotted period. Grants on the other hand are 'free' money and do not have to be paid back but there are invariably strict conditions as to how the grant aid is to be used.

In Britain there are dozens upon dozens of loan and grant schemes available for small businesses and business start-ups. They vary very much with geography and in the Government Aid status of the area where one lives. It has been said on a number of occasions that the loan and grant schemes in the UK are deliberately made as difficult and convoluted as possible in order to winnow out the less deserving cases. Grant and loan application procedures have been likened to bureaucratic obstacle courses.

The Training and Enterprise Companies, TEC's, (Local Enterprise Companies, LEC's in Scotland) should be your first port of call to find out what schemes are available in your area. Most of these organisations will have business counselling services available, usually free of charge, which can help you find the most appropriate package for your needs. It is very important to realise that virtually all of these grant and loan schemes are not retrospective. If you have already bought some hardware you are most unlikely to subsequently get any kind of grant or loan to cover the cost. In that unfortunate situation you will only be able to apply for aid in the form of working capital.

For those living in rural areas, especially in Wales and Scotland, pay particular attention to the many special schemes funded directly by the EEC. The EEC is very keen on seeing teleworking develop on the European rim and have a number of aid programmes directed at teleworking.

While it has already been touched on in Chapter 6, one should not overlook the clearing banks when looking for financial support. In spite of what sometimes are appearances to the contrary, they are, after all, in the business of lending money. But these days they are, and with good reason, looking at every new loan application through a magnifying glass and the success of any such application will depend entirely on your own credibility and that of your business plan.

Fortunately, the average teleworker will not be seeking vast amounts of money to get up and running. As was indicated in Chapter 1, a basic system can be set up for less than £3,000, while £4,000 can buy a very potent set-up. However, that can seem a fairly daunting sum to many people and it has to be said that most lenders want to see some financial commitment on the part of the borrower. As a general rule, lenders will match every pound put up by the proposer. This obstacle can be surmounted but it may require some hard decisions and a long cool look at all one's assets. Nevertheless, there is no better way to show one's commitment to a prospective lender than by having made some personal sacrifices in order to get your project of the ground.

A good business counsellor can prove invaluable in putting together a financial package tailored to suit one's individual needs.

In concluding this section, it must again be said that whatever scheme is put together, it is vital to maintain a dialogue on your progress with your lenders, whoever they may be.

CONTRACTS

Throughout this book there has been a continuing emphasis for the teleworker to adopt a totally professional approach to business. An integral part of this approach is the need to establish the contractual framework in which to do business. For the prospective teleworker, contractual arrangements may have to cover employment, standard conditions for working for third parties and any service contracts for the maintenance of equipment.

With respect to employment, a contract of employment is made as soon as a job has been offered and accepted. This can be done verbally although it is customary for the verbal agreement to be confirmed in writing. Once the contract has been made, the employer is required by law to give all employees working more than 16 hours per week written details of the main terms and conditions of their employment within 13 weeks of the commencement of that employment.

Every contract of employment must identify the parties involved, specify the date when employment began, and if the

employment is for a fixed period, the expiry date of the period. In addition, the contract must also state:

- the rate of pay or how the pay is worked out, and the pay period, (hourly, weekly, monthly, etc.);

- any rules as to hours of work, and if appropriate, a statement of what are normal working hours;

- entitlement to holidays, including public holidays and rates of holiday pay;

- rules on sickness or injury absence and sick pay;

- details of pension or pension scheme and whether the employee's employment in contracted-out of the State pension scheme;

- the length of notice the employee must give and is entitled to receive:

- the employee's job title;

- reference to any disciplinary rules affecting the employee;

- a person, identified by name or title to whom the employee can apply if he or she is dissatisfied with any disciplinary decision;

- a person, identified by name or title to whom the employee can take any job grievance.

At this time there are comparatively few conventionally employed teleworkers and it is likely that for the teleworker such a contract will be expanded to cover such matters as care of the employer's property, security, data protection and insurances. It is important that all employees know their rights and have a contract of employment. If you have any doubts about any clauses in a contract of employment, do check with a lawyer before you sign anything. In the brave new world of teleworking, both employer and employee will have to show some flexibility.

For the self-employed teleworker, it will pay to have drawn up a set of 'Standard Conditions of Contract'. These can either be drawn up by your lawyer or pro-forma conditions can be obtained from a number of professional bodies. These conditions are usually sub-divided into General Conditions and Fee Arrangements.

General conditions cover such matters as commercial confidentiality, professional indemnification, copyright expenses and any delays in completion of the work. Fee arrangements should cover the period of validity of any quotation, the method of monitoring work, how often invoices will be issued and the credit period allowed. For longterm contracts there must be a clause to allow for the periodic review of the contractual conditions and a revision of fees. There should also be a statement as to whether or not VAT will be charged.

Before commencing a contract both parties should sign and retain a specific contract covering all the salient features of the Standard Conditions of Contract. Always ensure that your contractual agreements are kept in a safe place, ideally with your bank or lawyer.

Service and maintenance contracts are dealt with in a later section.

PURCHASING

For those of you who have decided you use either an Apple Mac or an Acorn computer life is fairly straightforward. You select the model and configuration you require and then approach one of the many Apple Authorised Resellers or Acorn dealers. Shopping around will not produce any significant variations in price, since both Apple and Acorn closely monitor how their dealers trade and ensure that the recommended retail prices are closely adhered to. Points to watch when you are buying by mail order are covered in some detail later.

Selecting, never mind purchasing an IBM PC or clone is much more difficult, and can be a veritable minefield for the unwary. It has not been this book's policy to recommend any particular brand of hardware or software and it does not intend to do so now. What it will try to do is guide the beginner so that he or she makes the right choice and point out the potential pitfalls for the uninitiated.

We will assume at this stage that one has decided on the specification of a PC which will meet your teleworking requirements. The first decision is whether you want to go for one of the major brand names, such as IBM, Compaq, Olivetti and Apricot, a privilege one used to pay dearly for, or go for a lesser known brand at a much more competitive price. Both IBM and Compaq have recently reacted to the current price war and each has introduced a subsidiary brand of inexpensive PCs. IBM's new models carry the Ambra name while Compaq's are called the ProLinea PC range.

To see what alternatives are available one just has to buy one of the many PC oriented computer magazines. PC Magazine, Personal Computer World and Computer Buyer are among the most comprehensive with some worthwhile reading amongst all the advertisements In comparing the offerings of various glossy advertisements, it is essential to ensure that one compares like with like. Many advertisements leave out bits of information, usually it has to be said, to mask areas where corners are being cut in order to keep the price down. Particular areas to watch are the video card RAM and the standard and resolution of the supplied monitor. A complete list of all the essential technical parameters of a PC specification, is given in Appendix 4, and also covers other points such as whether the DOS is installed, a mouse and 'Windows' is included, delivery costs and what after-sales service is provided. It also specifies a basic system, a median system for 'Windows' and what might be called a power users system.

A major problem with many of the lesser known makes of PC clones is that it is virtually impossible to go to a shop or showroom to look at them and actually try them out. The only substitute is to read up the numerous 'group tests' of comparable PCs regularly published in the computer magazines. Alternatively, ask around your own area and find out who uses what. You cannot beat a personal recommendation.

The actual purchasing should be quite straightforward. You have selected a brand, made out a detailed specification and placed your order by mail or by visiting the dealer. You then drive off with the packages or eagerly await the delivery van. Unfortunately it is not always quite so simple. The computer does not appear to work, is delivered late or, horror of horrors, is not delivered at all.

In the UK, Consumer Rights as they are usually known, are embraced by a number of laws that collectively define the rights of the individual as a buyer. They vary slightly depending on whether you live in England and Wales, Scotland or Northern Ireland. There are two key points governing any transaction you have with a trader. The first is that the goods must fit any description that you are given and the second is that they must be of 'merchantable quality'. The Sale of Goods Act states that these two conditions are implied every time one makes a purchase, even if one just picks up an article, takes it to the cash point and pays for it. Every sale is a contract, so if any of the conditions are broken, the contract has been broken and you have recourse to action, either replacement of the defective item or your money back.

Most people in Britain now know the consumer protection that goes with making purchases with a credit or charge card. It certainly makes sense, if you are purchasing by mail order, to use this facility if you have it. It is invaluable if the supplier has ceased trading between receiving your order and it being dispatched. If you have sent a cheque you will have little chance of getting your money back, but do make sure your card has enough credit to allow you to make what can be a pretty large purchase.

A common and worrisome problem with mail order purchasing is late delivery. Try to ascertain when the goods will be dispatched when you place the order. Sometimes there will be a perfectly justifiable delay while the item is made to order or has to come from the manufacturer. If you feel there is an unseemly delay, call the supplier to find out what is happening, but do be polite and keep your cool. If the goods simply fail to appear and you feel your are being given the run around, contact the credit card company and your local Trading Standards Officer at your local council offices.

With regard to personal computers, the first thing to do on its arrival is to thoroughly check the outer packaging for any physical damage before you sign the receipt. The next is to carefully unpack the various components and try to verify by inspection that they match the items that have been ordered. Check off each item against the delivery note, and do not forget to see that all the various instruction manuals have been included. If there are any discrepancies, something missing or different from what was ordered or anything does not seem to be quite as it should be, telephone the supplier immediately, noting the time of the call, who was spoken to, and the nature of your complaint. Always retain all the boxes and other packaging materials in case something has to be returned to the supplier.

Connecting up the components of a personal computer is no more difficult than setting up a video cassette reorder. Take plenty of time to read the computer's user manual and identify all the components and their respective connecting leads. Find out if the DOS has been installed, as the start-up procedure is different if it's not. (Always ask the supplier to install the DOS before the computer is delivered.) Follow the manual's instructions to the letter and when you have everything ready, switch on. When personal computers are first switched on, they carry out what is called a Power On Self Test, POST. When the POST is successfully completed, what appears next on the screen depends on whether you have an Apple, an Acorn or a PC.

With an Apple Macintosh, the computer produces some bleeps when first switched on and the first thing to appear on the screen is a character called 'Mac'. If Mac has a smiling face all is well, if he has a sad face, the system has a problem and you must contact the dealer. A few seconds after the 'happy Mac' has appeared the screen will show a caption "Welcome to Macintosh" and the next screen picture will depend on how the operating system is configured.

With a PC, a number of cryptic messages will scroll on to the screen as the computer goes through its POST. If 'Windows' has been installed it will probably have been set up as a 'Terminate and Stay Resident', TSR, program and you will see the 'Windows' logo appear followed by the 'Windows' opening menu, Program Manager. Without 'Windows' you will see C:\, the ubiquitous DOS prompt sitting at the top left hand corner of the screen.

On the Acorn or Archimedes computers, the POST proceeds with a blank screen and an absence of sound other than that of the disk drives and when completed the Acorn icon bar appears across the bottom of the screen. The number and type of icons displayed depends on how the computer has been configured.

So what if it just does not work? Other than checking again that all the leads are properly connected, do not interfere with anything. Contact the supplier by phone, noting the time, date and the name of the person your are talking to. Above all, be courteous; ranting and raving down the telephone is always counter-productive, no matter how you may feel. Be firm, but remember that courtesy and diplomacy will win more battles than aggression and abuse. If all else fails contact the Trading Standards Office or the Citizen's Advice Bureau, although it is worth noting that some of the computer magazines operate a helpline for dealing with recalcitrant suppliers.

SERVICE AND MAINTENANCE

To the teleworker operating out in the sticks, good service and maintenance arrangements are vital. A number of computer and peripheral manufacturers are already using specialist third party companies to provide their warranty cover and on-site maintenance service.

To most teleworkers the most important clause in any maintenance agreement will cover the 'response time', the time it will take between the teleworker making a call and the service engineer turning up at your premises. As with most things, you get what you pay for. A 24 hour, seven day a week, call out service will cost more than one that undertakes to get someone to you the next working day. It is also important to appreciate that any computer engineer's efficiency is largely bound up with the amount of spares he carries, or at least kept in store by his company.

Before signing any maintenance contract do some homework. Check that the company is financially sound and that you are fully conversant with the computer and peripherals that you have. Ask for some references and do not shy from taking them up. If you have any doubts on any of the more obscure clauses in the company's contract, get your lawyer to check it over before you sign anything.

In Britain, the simplest way to find a computer maintenance company will be in your local "Yellow Pages". Be sure to ask for some existing customer references before engaging anyone. The best possible recommendation for any service is a satisfied customer. Always get a written quotation before authorising any work and a receipt for your PC before it and your data are removed from your premises.

The teleworker will have to strike a balance between having adequate protection in the event of disaster and the cost of that protection. After a warranty period has elapsed, the teleworker may have grown in confidence to such an extent that further outlay does not seem worthwhile. A less expensive option can be to take out insurance cover. Some may feel the risks are so small that no formal cover is necessary and simply rely on calling a maintenance company out as and when the need arises. The disadvantage of this ad-hoc approach is that your call might not be given the same priority as one from someone who has a conventional service contract.

An advantage of the PC is its modular construction which means that a defective component can be readily replaced by another one. This is all very well for things like floppy disk drives and graphic cards but remember that if your hard disk ever fails, it contains all your invaluable data, so once again make sure you adopt a systematic approach to backing up all your data. The modular nature of the PC was a contributory factor in causing the Granada company to move into the field of computer servicing, which they saw as a logical extension to their nationwide coverage of TV and VCR maintenance.

BOOKS AND ACCESSORIES

It has been frequently stated in this book that many of the manuals that accompany software packages are not very intelligible and often written in dreadful English. As a result a number of specialist publishers now cater exclusively for this lucrative and expanding market. Que, Sybex, Bantam and Ziff-Davis are the leading publishers in this field, with books covering every facet of computers and computing.

The teleworker should be selective in his or her choice of books. Books do of course vary in quality and are targeted at different levels of user. The computer magazines usually publish monthly book reviews which should help you make the right selection. The author would recommend that to begin with one should restrict oneself to a comprehensive manual on your chosen operating system and an intermediate level manual for each of the application programmes that have been chosen. For PC users, a good additional purchase might be 'The PC Configuration Handbook' by John Woram (Bantam) which is a good introduction into what goes on under the bonnet of your PC.

Sooner or later the teleworker is going to want at least some of a vast number of the accessories that are made for the computer user market, or simply needs to replace comsumables such as floppy disks, paper and printer ink or ribbon. Three companies, Action, Inmac and Misco operate mail order businesses offering a huge range of computer peripherals and accessories. They each offer a service that could be described as being almost tailor-made for the teleworker and usually combine good pricing with a next day delivery unless you live in the Highlands and Islands. The Action catalogue is particularly useful in that they also stock a wide range of software, with all the big names well represented.

Like it or not we are now all living in the Information Age. For just a few hundred pounds anyone can buy a personal computer which can sit on a desktop and has a number crunching ability that would have cost millions of pounds thirty years ago and filled a house. Programmers have progressively devised application software that can readily put into practice without the operator requiring several years experience and a good Ph.D.

These tools, with a little help from a modem and the telephone companies can put quite extraordinary capabilities into millions of hands. Hopefully, this book has shown that the concept of teleworking can make some of these capabilities a reality, and be of real benefit to our national, corporate and individual lives.

Teleworking is still in its infancy, and in the next, concluding chapter, we shall take a brief look into the future and consider how teleworking and the computer are going to increasingly affect our lifestyles.

10 Into the Future

Anyone who has dipped into the past and read an article or book predicting what our world and life would be like twenty or thirty years hence will have realised that most of these prophesies have been somewhat fanciful and over-ambitious. In spite of some quite extraordinary technological developments, life for most of us is not so dramatically different from what it was thirty-odd years ago. But the overall rate of change has clearly speeded up during the past decade. This section endeavours to make some realistic predictions on what life might be like at the beginning of the twenty-first century, with particular reference to developments in teleworking.

TELECOMMUNICATIONS

The telephone, or perhaps more accurately the telephone networks will be the cornerstone of progress here, and there will be two main thrusts to this future development. One will be an overall increase in the provision of telephone lines; usage in the EEC as a whole is less than 50 percent per household or business at present, although there are considerable national differences. The second will be the continued change from electro-mechanical to digital technology. The EEC is well ahead of the rest of the world here with, in 1990, about 35 percent of the networks being digital; this compares well to the USA at 20 percent and Japan, surprisingly with only 5 percent.

Needless to say, all the national phone companies (PTTs) are well aware of the enormous potential for growth in their industry. The PTTs however will not have things all their own way. Many other utility providers, notably railway and water companies, are planning to set up telecommunication networks alongside their existing services. Setting up such networks beside railway tracks, canals, pipelines and so on will cause minimal disruption to the existing infrastructure. It remains to be seen whether these newcomers to the telecoms business will operate these new networks themselves or rent them out to PTTs, cable TV companies or large corporations wishing to rent their own high capacity data transmission lines.

The progressive 'digitisation' of the telephone networks means a much wider availability of Integrated Services Digital Network or ISDN lines. ISDN are limited to all-digital links and at present their use is limited to specialised high speed data transmission. Their potential is immense, since they offer the capacity to handle voice, fax, computer and video traffic on the same telephone line. This is likely to lead to the development of a multi-purpose 'telecom' terminal which will offer some or all of a range of communication, information and media services.

Growth in mobile telephones will continue apace with a gradual shift to digital radio technology which will, on the one hand, provide pan-European coverage and, on the other, eliminate unauthorised eavesdropping using scanning radio receivers. Costs of both instruments and rental will be progressively reduced to encourage more widespread non-business use and eventually the only charges will be for calls made.

At present telephone charges are made to a base number, be it fixed or mobile. Eventually this will change with the introduction of 'smart cards' known as Subscriber Identity Modules (SIM). All forms of device using the telephone networks will ultimately have a card 'wipe' facility, and charges will be billed to the individual subscriber, irrespective of what service has been used or from where the call was made. Quite apart from helping businesses control their costs, this facility could well be regarded as a godsend by the parents of teenage children, to whom cards could be given with a very modest credit limit!

INFORMATION TECHNOLOGY

Until now IT and the computer have been virtually synonymous. The next decade will see the progressive integration of all the recognised sources of information, the computer, telephone, television together with many facets of what we refer to as 'the media'.

While many business executives already feel that they are being overwhelmed by an avalanche of often conflicting information, they have, to use a well-known phrase, "ain't seen nothin' yet". In the future, the IT professional will not be concerned with the technology of collecting information; his or her main task will be to ensure that only the most relevant information is selected and then presented to the management of the enterprise or organisation in a way that it can be readily assimilated and understood, all in the shortest possible time.

This will be easier said than done. There are examples in the recent past of some industries, which many would regard as being at the cutting edge of IT, banking, high street retailing and insurance readily come to mind, having unexpectedly catastrophic financial results. The problem is rarely the quantity or quality of information; it is either the inability to separate fact from opinion, or more often the failure to identify the really crucial information and to react to it.

How organisations will tackle this fundamental problem is not clear at this time. Some will hive off or 'privatise' their IT function to a third party specialist. There will be a growth in the number of companies offering industry specific databases or information retrieval services. Both offer considerable opportunities to the teleworker. In-depth appreciation of IT and its ever widening ramifications will be an essential component in the make up of the successful manager in the twenty-first century.

ENTERPRISE AND MANAGEMENT

Once again, small is beautiful. While many different types of enterprise will continue to operate on a global basis we are already seeing the start of a rigorous re-appraisal in the way the large multi-nationals structure their enterprise and do business. There are several reasons for this. Recession has concentrated the corporate mind wonderfully and the need to respond faster to changes in the marketplace, environmental awareness and a changing world order have all played their part. Size equates to mass and mass critically affects momentum on the one hand and inertia on the other. IT shrinks both distance and time and the successful enterprises of the next century are going to have to be uncommonly fast on their feet.

Some of the more progressive and far-sighted companies are already well on their way. Glaxo, one of Britain's largest and most successful companies already has a management structure in place where any plant manager, anywhere in the world is only two intermediaries away from the company chairman. Shortening the lines of command, nationally and internationally can dramatically reduce a company's response times with a corresponding improvement in its competitive advantage.

Notwithstanding the continued impact of automation, there will be an inexorable decrease in the number of people working on one site, be it a factory or 'office'. Smaller numbers can mean a greater 'esprit', promote team identity, offer greater flexibility and better job satisfaction, all vital ingredients in achieving that elusive objective, Total Quality Management. There will be winners and losers in this transformation. The most conspicuous losers are going to be middle management. The old fashioned head office will be ruthlessly whittled down to its essential functions; corporate perks and largesse will largely disappear. The winners will be multi-skilled operatives working in a more stimulating way and often in more convivial surroundings.

Middle managers should not feel too despondent after reading the rather bleak prognosis for them in the previous paragraph. These projected changes represent job re-deployment rather than wholesale job losses. The tele-age will offer as many new opportunities as it does redundancies. Those with foresight will survive and prosper. As a first step, if you are not already keyboard and computer literate, start learning now, and start to think about teleworking!

The Chief Executive Officer of the next century is going to be more the visionary, less the whizz kid. He or she will be concentrating on the big picture while subordinates do the day-to-day chores. Above all, especially in Britain, they will need to think long term. This may seem anomalous advice for what will be times of change. But British enterprise has all too frequently been handicapped by the short term needs of its owners, be they individual shareholders or institutions, and its lenders, the British banking system. We only have to compare Britain's industrial performance over the past twenty years with that of Japan and Germany to see the folly of short termism.

Growth will also become a relic of the past. We have become used to seeing companies enjoying periods of amazing growth followed almost inevitably by equally rapid and sometimes terminal decline. Many institutional investors regard growth as the most significant yardstick of success. One of the great challenges of the twenty-first century and a key to real economic and environmental stability will be the emergence of companies who can thrive in a 'steady state' condition; adapting, renewing, re-positioning, changing their products and markets while maintaining their 'size' and level of economic activity.

THE WORKPLACE

The paperless office was always a mirage. While more and more information will be obtained from and stored in computers there is a limit as to how much of it can be readily assimilated directly from a VDU. There will always be a need for executive summaries, reports and so forth. Many traditional office jobs will be spun off to smaller out-offices, others to teleworkers. But personal contact will have to be maintained, whether it be in-company or between the company and its customers. Some meetings will be replaced by teleconferencing but in many spheres there will still be a need for face to face contact. Offices are likely to be much more informal and openly structured places with homeworkers periodically going into the office for lunch and a chat with colleagues.

In the factory, automation will continue and production units will become more specialised. There will be increasing polarisation into manufacturers and assemblers. Production line boredom will be alleviated by team or group work practices and the continual need to change product specifications to meet the varying requirements of national or niche markets. 'Mass produced customisation' will be the order of the day, with the production line responding almost hour by hour to the changing demands of the marketplace, wherever it might be.

Factories themselves will progressively become smaller and increasingly 'worker friendly' to compensate for increasingly high capital costs and a trend to-round-the-clock working. Demographic changes will put increasing pressure on companies to attract and retain progressively more skilled and valuable workforces and a whole range of on-site services such as child minding, electronic shopping and banking, training, further education and medical schemes will become the norm.

EDUCATION

Most schools in Europe and North America now boast at least one personal computer. Some have a fully equipped and staffed computing department. So far however, very little has been done by the educationalists to take advantage of the computer as a teaching aid. Computing, computer science and Information Technology are widely taught in secondary and high schools but as yet, very little teaching of other subjects is done using the computer.

So far, television has made a much greater impact and many Universities in Canada and the USA have been selling course modules on video for several years now. Students can draw a particular tape from the library and go over it as often as they like and the video lectures are supported by sets of course notes or textbooks. There is no good reason why schools should not enhance there income by marketing and selling the skills of their best teachers in a similar way. This use of television will continue with the eventual provision of dedicated education channels, with, in the UK, the Open University being complemented by the Open School.

Educationalists and teachers have barely scratched the surface of computing as a teaching aid. The introduction of the GUI has largely removed the need for keyboard literacy. The CDROM and CD-I offer undreamed of opportunities for education. Imagine a whole high school syllabus such as 'A' level Maths, complete with interactive questions and answers on one compact disc – it is already possible.

In San Francisco and Chicago pioneering work is already underway with groups of schools linked on a WAN and in one case individual pupils linked to the school and each other. School staff use the networks to share course preparation work while the pupils communicate amongst themselves as part of projects or simply to help each other with homework!

The teaching profession will no doubt look on such developments with a mixture of disbelief and abject horror. It is certainly possible, although highly improbable, to extrapolate such a vision to the point where the school as we know it is just a glorified child-minding service and those who really wish to study will do so in front of some kind of VDU or TV set at home, with many attending school only for the odd tutorial or to sit examinations.

Many will scoff at such a scenario but the teachers ignore the scope of the computer and information technology at their peril. All is not gloom; it will take millions of men and women hours to compile and update these new types of educational materials, and virtually all of the work lends itself to teleworking. To still be a teacher and yet not having ever to face a pupil or a classroom again may prove an irresistible attraction to many!

THE HOME

Like it or not, many of us are going to spend a good deal more time in our homes than we do at present. How we spend that time will be very much up to individual choice; we need not degenerate into a nation of couch potatoes. Some, having read thus far, will be invigorated by the prospect of new horizons and challenges, others may find this view of the next century manifestly depressing. But as always, life will be what each of us makes of it. Yes, there will be losers as well as winners, but hopefully, and this writer is hopeful, given the already massive re-organisation and re-deployment of industry that Britain has coped with over the past thirty years, the losers will be very much in the minority.

Home life, be it work or leisure, will centre round the instrument at the end of the telephone line, currently called a telephone. In the future it will be much more than that. It will have sockets for the television, the computer and the fax machine. It will probably have a card 'wipe' facility for either paying for calls or for charge card and credit card purchases. Some versions will have their own small TV screen for video-conferencing or video-calling.

Teleworking, both in the home or from small satellite offices will become a much more widely accepted way of working, although it is unrealistic to expect teleworking to become the rule rather than the exception. House design will progressively change to provide purpose designed workspace for one or more members of the family as well as incorporating the latest energy conservation measures and the use of more environmentally sympathetic materials.

The home environment will increasingly come under computer control. Heating, cooking, lighting and even drawing the curtains will all be programmable or else controlled remotely while you are out of the house or on holiday, not to mention permanent on-line intruder protection. More purchasing than ever will be done by mail order, and just replacing the bulky mail order catalogue by a disc for a CD-ROM, will take some of the pressure off the world's forests.

THE ENVIRONMENT

In one of their informative reports on Teleworking (4) B.T. Research Laboratories concluded that the most significant result from a transfer from conventional office work to teleworking would be from the consequent decrease in commuting. In national terms, the savings are small, a 0.06 percent reduction of the UK energy budget for every 1 percent of jobs transferred. However the individual worker will experience significant savings in transport costs.

Summing up, B.T. concludes "Thus, whilst it would be wrong to present teleworking as a major way of improving the environment, it is clear that this method of working does have some environmental advantage over that based on a centralised workplace. In the future, adoption of teleworking could reduce the need for new office buildings as well as reduce energy consumption and thus form part of a long term strategy to reduce consumption of both energy and other raw materials."

Teleworking will at least contribute to the stabilisation of carbon dioxide emissions if not radically reduce them. It is in inner city life that the widespread adoption of teleworking will make the greatest impact, by the progressive reduction in the numbers working in the prototypical city centre office. Hugely expensive expansion of the roads network and public transport can be reduced and the quality of life for the city dweller greatly improved. Another longer term benefit might be the 'recycling' of redundant office buildings into housing, thus increasing the housing stock without further erosion of the green belt. Such views will be anathema to the banks and the property speculators, but they will certainly make good sense to the homeless and the environmental lobby.

In global terms it is all too easy to think of the 'environment' as somebody else's problem. While international co-operation and commitment is still some way off, there is now no doubt that man's profligacy can and does seriously damage our planet and many of its creatures. The 'Greens' do have a case, but so far that case has been flawed by their inability to put up any credible alternatives. Individual efforts barely scratch the surface of the problem. Unfortunately, homo sapiens' track record in facing such difficulties is not a good one, all too often delaying the application of what is a remarkable intellect until the fifty-ninth minute of the twelfth hour.

For a start, this simplistic writer wonders why it seems to be beyond the wit of man to build large ozone factories in some suitable locations to replace the parts of the layer we have wantonly depleted, or to seriously start to harness the most abundant and cleanest energy of all – geothermal. Wind generators may be green, but my goodness, they are a blight on the landscape.

Appendix 1

A Brief History of the Electronic Computer

BOOLE & TURING

The first foundations of the theory of modern computing were unwittingly laid down in the mid-nineteenth century by a self-taught Lincolnshire schoolmaster, George Boole (1815–1864). Boole devised a mathematical theory which showed how some mathematical problems could be expressed in symbols. These symbols could them be manipulated without changing the logic of the original problem, provided that all the factors in the problem could be expressed by variables that had only two states. Boole called these two states; true or false. Using this 'Boolean' approach frequently clarified a problem enough to aid its solution. With his theory, Boole changed the study of logic from an art to a science.

The basic principles of what was to be the modern computer were set out in 1936 by the English mathematician Alan Turing (1912–1954). Turing was able to show, using a very complicated mathematical proof that one simple machine could, using only three computable functions – addition, subtraction and comparison, solve many algebraic and mathematical problems. Turing's hypothetical machine consisted of a unit to perform the calculations, he referred to it as an 'automaton' and a form of data storage; he proposed punched paper tape. Data could be stored on the tape, but only using three symbols, zeros, ones and full stops. The 'automaton' could read symbols from, write symbols to, or delete symbols from the portion of tape under its read-or-write head. It could also move the tape one space backwards or forwards.

The key to Turing's hypothetical machine was the provision of a unique sequence of steps, an 'algorithm', to solve the problem. Up to that time, mathematicians had thought that different machines would be required to solve different problems.

A further vital step leading to the building of the first electronic computers was made in 1938 by Claude Shannon, a research assistant at the Massachusetts Institute of Technology. Shannon demonstrated that binary devices such as a relay or a thermionic valve could completely emulate 'Bolean logic', and thus paved the way for the construction of the first computers using available technology.

WARTIME DEVELOPMENTS

The outbreak of the second World War provided the catalyst for the construction of the first computers. Work proceeded simultaneously, but quite independently, in Germany, Britain and the United States, in different circumstances and with different objectives.

Konrad Zuse a German design engineer built four computers, Z1 – Z4 during the period 1936–1944. Although he worked in isolation and received absolutely no state aid from the German Reich, Zuse's computers were far more advanced than the other wartime machines, a remarkable achievement. They were electro-mechanical and were constructed in Zuse's parents' home, using little more than Meccano and second-hand telephone relays. We are perhaps fortunate that the regimented attitudes that permeated the Third Reich did not appreciate the far-reaching implications of Zuse's work. His Z3 machine was used during the war by the Henschel Aircraft Company to speed up calculations on airframe design. One of his machines, Z4 survived the war and a replica of Z3 is in the Deutches Museum in Munich.

In Britain, the first truly electronic computer, Colossus 1 was built in 1943 to a design by Turing, Flowers and Newman. It was constructed with the express purpose of helping to decode intercepted German radio messages. Several accounts of this fascinating project have been published elsewhere. Suffice it to say that the success of the Bletchley Park codebreakers in shaping the outcome of the Second World War, fully justified the effort put into creating Colossus 1 and its successors; they were undoubtedly the world's first successful electronic computers.

The Colossus machines were built using thermionic valves, 1,500 in Colossus 1, which could switch on and off much faster than the mechanical relays used in Zuse's machines. Small changes to the computers' program could be made through switches in the front panel of the machines, but more extensive changes required rewiring. Data for analysis was fed into the machine using punched paper tape, which the machine could read, using a photo-electric cell, at the remarkable rate of 5,000 characters per second. Altogether, 11 Colossus machines were built but none are known to have survived to the present day.

In the United States of America, two separate approaches were underway. One was to prove a technological dead-end but was to be the foundation of the IBM company's long held domination of the computer world; the second was a technological breakthrough that helped to ensure that, for the next 30 years, the computer world would be centred in the United States.

In 1936, Howard H. Aiken, an associate professor of mathematics at Harvard University began to wonder if it would be possible to combine into one large general purpose computer a number of the successful mechanical calculators that were then available. Aiken quickly realised that such a machine would have to be designed from scratch and would require considerable technical and financial resources. IBM was already a successful company making mechanical calculators and was run at that time by the irascible and autocratic Thomas J. Watson. Aiken had prepared a convincing case indicating the commercial benefits of such a machine, the Automatic Sequence Controlled Calculator, ASCC, and approached Watson for support. Watson quickly agreed to fund the project, at which point war broke out.

Aiken was quickly enlisted into the US Navy, and was soon explaining to his superiors the nature of his ASCC project. They immediately saw its relevance to a number of naval matters and Aiken was released on secondment to continue the project. The design work was done at Harvard and the manufacture and assembly carried out at IBM's headquarters at Endicott, NY. The ASCC was tested in 1943 after which it was stripped down for modification and reassembly at Harvard. The Harvard Mk 1 as it was called was a huge machine, 50 feet long, 8 feet high and about 6 feet deep, containing about one million components. At Watson's insistence, great care had been taken with the machines appearance; it was meticulously laid out and clad in stainless steel and glass, in marked contrast to the ad-hoc and hasty construction of the other early computers. In spite of its impressive appearance, the ASCC, being electro-mechanical, was an extremely slow device, even the first electronic machines being over one thousand times faster. At the end of the war, Watson sanctioned the building of an improved version, but the purely electronic machines rendered this obsolete before it was completed. Nevertheless, the name of IBM was already at the forefront of computer manufacture.

The second prong of the American assault into the realms of computing took place at the Moore School of Engineering in Pennsylvania. The project began at a request from the military for an extremely rapid calculator to deal with the many complex calculations needed to compile ballistic tables for new guns and missiles. After considerable thought, two of the Moore School staff, Mauchly and Eckert, put forward in 1942 a proposal for general purpose computer called an Electronic Numerical Integrator and Calculator, ENIAC, utilising the high speed switching power of the thermionic valve. Construction of ENIAC took two and a half years and it was first switched on in February 1946. ENIAC was also a huge machine, over 100 feet long and weighing more than 30 tons. It contained more than 19,000 valves and consumed more than 2,000 kilowatts of electricity. ENIAC was externally programmed using plugboards to set up a sequence of operations to solve a problem, while data input and output was through punched cards.

While ENIAC had more flexibility than Colossus, it had after all been designed as a general purpose calculator while Colossus was specifically to aid code breaking, it was still difficult, in spite of the plugboards, to switch it from one task to another and some parts of the machine had to be rewired. In basic terms, the power of these early computers could be measured in terms of three factors, speed, capacity and, for want of a better word, flexibility. The Colossus machines were powerful with regard to speed and capacity but very weak on flexibility; they could only help to crack codes. ENIAC was even more powerful in terms of speed and capacity, but still, in spite of its general purpose tag, relatively weak in terms of flexibility.

The final breakthrough came about from a chance meeting at a railway station in 1945 between one of the engineers on the ENIAC project Herman Goldstine, and the world-famous mathematician John von Neumann (1903–1957). Both men knew each other and had very high security clearances. From the ensuing conversation von Neumann first learnt of ENIAC and his extraordinary mind quickly realised that the computer had far wider implications than the nuclear weapons on which he was working at that time.

Shortly afterwards, Von Neumann joined the ENIAC project as a consultant and soon produced a report that contained the first clear description of the stored program and the modern computer.

Von Neumann realised that ENIAC was limited by its relative inflexibility but rather than speeding up the process of feeding program to the computer, he proposed that the programs be stored inside the computer itself rather than in some external system. In a stored program computer, the computer finds out which operation is to be carried out next by looking at its own memory. This concept was the final piece in the creation of the framework of the electronic computer as we know it today. It meant that a computer program could be changed in a relatively simple way and led directly to the computer itself assisting in the preparation of programs whereby it can translate a program written in programming language into the code for the operations it actually performs.

ENIA's successor, the Electronic Discrete Variable Automatic Computer, EDVAC was completed in 1950 and was a fully fledged stored program computer.

With the end of the War, most of the shrouds of secrecy that had of necessity surrounded the early computers were torn away and commercial exploitation began in earnest. Britain's early lead, stored programme computers were working in Manchester, the Mk1, and Cambridge, the Electronic Delay Storage Automatic Calculator, ESDAC, early in 1949, was soon overtaken by the USA as the Americans, quick as ever to see the civil as well as the defense implications of the new technology, poured increasingly large sums of money into the new industry, investments that were to soon pay off handsomely.

Leaving aside the evolution of mechanical calculators, from the abacus via Schickard, Babbage and others to Hollerith, it had taken mankind about a hundred years to evolve the electronic computer. But these new-fangled computers were a complete mystery to most people. They were very large, very expensive, needed an air-conditioned environment and required highly trained operators. In the early fifties it was thought inconceivable that the computer would have any impact on the lives of ordinary people. In fact that was never going to be the case because in December 1947, at the laboratories of the Bell Telephone Company, three physicists had invented the device we now know as the transistor.

THE TRANSISTOR AND SOLID STATE ELECTRONICS

Bardeen, Brittan and Schockley received the 1956 Nobel Prize for Physics for what many regard as the "discovery of the century". The transistor is a small electric switch for electric current, and as it is based on the properties of a solid, crystalline semi-conductor, it is said to be a solid-state device. This contrasts with the older technology of the thermionic valve, in which a metal filament is heated in a gas contained by a glass envelope. This fundamentally new concept meant that transistors could progressively be made smaller and smaller and the technology moved forward to the extent that complete electrical circuits, and latterly multiple circuits could be made on one tiny piece of semi-conductor, usually silicon, hence the integrated circuit, the silicon chip and the micro chip. The most important spin-offs from this inexorable trend in miniaturisation were speed, cost and power consumption, since the smaller the transistor, the less current it uses.

ENIAC could carry out about 5,000 functions or instructions per second, and with the introduction of transistor based computers, this rose to 100,000 instructions per second. Today, computer speeds are measured in Millions of Instructions Per Second, MIPS.

It took twelve years for the transistor to be developed sufficiently for it to be incorporated into a computer. These so-called "second generation" computers also benefited from continuing development in memory and data transfer systems, punched cards and paper tape being progressively replaced by magnetic tape, floppy disks, and then hard disks, with the capacity and performance of each type being continually enhanced until superseded by new technology.

These second generation computers were still very large and expensive machines, occupying large air-conditioned rooms and lovingly tended by large teams of acolytes whose skills were shrouded in mystery. The introduction of solid state technology had not yet produced any reduction in scale. Initial gains from miniaturisation were more than offset by the need for greater speed and performance. These large computers soon became known as mainframes, and their uses were confined mainly to the military, government departments and the very large industrial corporations.

Further miniaturisation of electronic components continued during the late sixties and seventies and resulted in further advances in computer hardware.

The integrated circuit, IC, was created in which hundreds of solid state devices were fitted on to a single silicon chip about one centimetre square.

It was the next step in this continuing trend in downsizing that produced the breakthrough which led to the explosive expansion in the use of computers. Very Large Scale Integration, VLSI, made it possible to incorporate thousands, and ultimately hundreds of thousands of solid state devices onto a single silicon chip. This technology lead directly to the invention of the two devices that were to revolutionise computer technology, the microprocessor and the solid state memory.

The first microprocessor, the Intel 4004 was produced in 1971. Its design team, led by Ted Hoff, were the first to realise that the electronics of a computer could be simplified if it were controlled by the software, in other words, that complexity in hardware and software were interchangeable. The 4004 could handle 4 bits of data at once, and had a speed of 100,000 hertz (or cycles per second). Its successor today can handle 32 bits of data at once at a speed of 50 Mhz (Megahertz or millions of cycles per second) a two thousandfold gain in performance.

There are a considerable number of semi-conductor memory devices and we shall confine ourselves here to the two basic types; read-only memories (ROM) and random access memories (RAM). ROMs as one would expect can only give a computer bits of information previously stored on it, while a RAM can both be read from and written to, and can thus accept from as well as give data to the computer. Memory chips were developed in parallel with microprocessor chips and are produced using the same technology. Memory chip development has not seemed quite so dramatic as that of microprocessors but they are a vital component in the overall cost of a computer which requires only one microprocessor but many memory chips, whose capacity crucially affects the computer's overall performance.

FROM MINI TO MICRO

Meanwhile the mainframe computer manufacturers had realised there was a demand for a smaller size of computer and in the mid-sixties the minicomputer was introduced. Minicomputers were about one tenth of the size of a mainframe and one tenth of the cost. These minis were not just smaller but they were becoming faster and much more reliable, not needing to be operated and maintained by computer experts. The manufacturers offered maintenance contracts and computer use spread into the business world as companies started to use them in offices and factories. The power of these minicomputers also permitted the introduction of multi-tasking, since the central processing unit (CPU) could carry out a number of separate tasks at the same time. This led directly to the multi-user system, Figure 1, whereby the central computer was accessed by a number of separate terminals, increasing both utilisation and productivity. Minicomputers are usually regarded as being third generation computers.

Early in 1975, an American electronics magazine gave details of how to build a small or microcomputer from a kit. This was the 'Altair' and used another Intel microprocessor, the 8080. This primitive machine was suitable only for enthusiasts or 'computer freaks' but it was the first computer cheap enough to be purchased by individuals. Thus the personal computer was born.

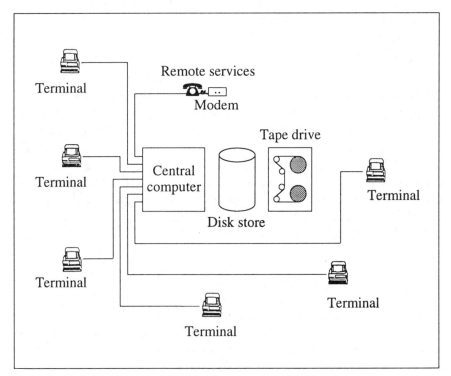

Figure 1

ENTER THE PERSONAL COMPUTER

The Apple Corporation was also started in 1975, by two computer freaks, Steve Wozniak and Steve Jobs, from a garage in California. The Apple 1 was followed in 1978 by the Apple 2, which quickly became established as the world's most popular computer mainly on account of it having the first sensible colour graphics system. Other electronic companies soon jumped on the accelerating bandwagon. These early personal computers used television sets as visual display units (VDU) and the program were loaded from audio tape cassettes.

The IBM company had missed out on the early development of microprocessors and personal computers and did not introduce its first microcomputer, the IBM PC until 1981. The IBM PC was not a revolutionary machine; IBM was not a company that took risks. Many of the components came from outside sources the microprocessor being Intel's 8088. The operating program or Disk Operating System (DOS) was bought from Microsoft, a deal that was the basis of that company's phenomenal growth. The IBM PC was just what the market wanted. It appealed to both people and companies who could begin to see the PC's relevance to business. With IBM's approval, the personal computer had become respectable and within a couple of years the PC had overtaken the Apple 2 to become the best selling microcomputer.

Surprisingly for a product from IBM, who normally plays its corporate cards exceedingly close to its chest, but inevitably given the nature of third party involvement, the PC was a relatively 'open' system. In no time at all, large numbers of look-alike 'clones' were being produced which were much cheaper than an IBM original. These varied from respectable look-alikes such as Compaq to some very dubious and inexpensive clones from South Korea and Taiwan.

In marked contrast, Apple kept its microprocessor production tightly controlled and its system well under wraps and its computers have always been fairly expensive; to this day there are no Apple clones. Apple Computer Inc. and its corporate development must now be a standard case study in every business school. This extraordinarily innovative company was the first to introduce quality colour graphics and then, in 1984 introduced the remarkable concept of the Graphical User Interface (GUI). The GUI removed much of the need to type in weird instructions from the keyboard, making the computer much easier for the uninitiated operator to use. Furthermore Apple always regarded text as a form of graphics making it much easier to combine words, drawings and exotic typestyles which led to Apple's domination of the fields of printing, publishing and graphic design.

In spite of all of these advantages, Apple has consistently failed to match sales of the IBM PC and its clones. Apple conspicuously failed to adopt the classical business strategy of reducing its prices once initial high margins had recovered development costs and increasing production rates brought economies of scale. Apple maintained its high margins for far too long and as a result, PCs have continually outsold Apples by about five to one. Recent estimates suggest that there are about 80 million PCs worldwide and about 15 million Apples.

Since their introduction both the PC and the Apple computers have been continually enhanced with more and more power being crammed into the same space and at prices which are lower in actual, never mind real terms. The transportable PC was introduced in the mid-eighties followed the battery powered 'notebook' computer a couple of years later.

NETWORKS

When the personal computer was in its infancy the business world was initially unconvinced and felt it had little use other than in a few specialist applications. This all changed with the advent of the network. Networks, known as LANs (Local Area Network) or WANs (Wide Areas Network) resulted from the transfer of the multi-user concept to the personal computer.

Both LANs and WANs come in three different flavours; the Star or Client-Server type, where each computer on the network is connected to the file-server in the centre, the Bus type, where the computers are each connected to a long common line known as a 'bus', and the 'Ring' type, where the 'bus' is joined into a circle.

The introduction of networks and networking transformed business attitudes to the personal computer. Suddenly, mainframe or mini computing power was readily and cheaply available, and personal computer sales went into orbit.

WORKSTATIONS AND SUPERCOMPUTERS

With the advent and burgeoning success of the personal computer, the 'traditional' manufacturers of computers soon felt the chill wind of change blowing through their industry. They reacted in a number of ways. One was to take on board the benefits of the integrated circuit and the microprocessor and to produce a range of computers known as 'superminis' which packed the power of the mainframe into a one metre cube. A second was to development extremely powerful desktop machines for use in the fast growing field of computer aided design and computer aided management, CAD-CAM. These were called 'workstations' and were usually four or five times more expensive than the top-of-the-range personal computers, although the differences in capability and price are continually narrowing. A third, highly specialised approach was the development of the 'supercomputer', a field dominated by the Cray company in the USA. These machines could carry out 250 MIPS and were used for highly sophisticated forms of CAD-CAM, notably in the aeronautical and motor car industries.

In the meantime, the microprocessor has, virtually unseen, permeated our lives in hundreds of different ways. Numerous everyday appliances either owe their very existence or their continuing refinement to the ubiquitous silicon chip. They are to be found in washing machines and video recorders, sewing machines and telephones, cars and cameras, to name but a few, while digital watches and pocket calculators have long been taken for granted.

Current research is dominated by attempts to create 'artificial intelligence' super supercomputers which will be able to learn and think. Notwithstanding the mind-blowing developments of the past twenty five years, computers are still somewhere short of replicating the most remarkable computer of all – the human brain.

Appendix 2
Useful Telephone Number

4th Dimension, ACI UK	0625 536178
Acorn Computer Ltd	0223 245200
ACRE	0285 653477
ACT II Ltd	0546 603828
Action Computer Supplies	0800 333333
Adobe, Principal Distribution	0706 831831
Advent	0793 511432
Aldus	031 220 4747
Apple Computer U.K. Ltd	081 569 1199
Apricot Computer	021 717 7799
ArchiCad, PRD	0902 755293
Asymetrix, No 1 Software	0604 830496
A.T.C. Telebureau	0691 89528
Autodesk U.K.	0483 303322
Banyan	0293 612284
Bitstream International	0242 227377
Borland	0734 320022

Canon U.K.	0800 252223
Central Point Software	081 848 1414
CIX	081 390 8446
Claris, Frontline Distribution	0256 20534
Colton Software	0954 211472
Compaq Computer Ltd	081 332 3000
Compuserve	0800 289378
Computer Associates	0753 577733
Commodore	0800 686868
Corel, Frontline Distribution	0256 20534
Dataease U.K.	081 554 0582
Data Protection Agency	0625 535777
Datastar	071 930 5503
DEC	0734 868711
Deepak Sareen	081 423 8855
Dell Computer Corporation Ltd	0344 720000
Delrina	081 207 3163
Dialog Europe	0865 326226
Digital Research	0344 860401
Dowty	0923 258000
EasiWriter	0533 546225
Epson	0442 261144
Euro Journal of Teleworking	0736 69477
European Software Publishers	0628 23453
Filemaker, Frontline Distribution	0256 20534
FT Profile	0932 761444

Freelance, Lotus	0784 455445
Genesis 2	0532 502615
Gravatom	0329 825757
Harvard Graphics, SPC	0344 867100
Hayes	0252 775500
Hewlett-Packard	0344 361263
IBM	0705 321212
ICC	081 783 1122
Info Select, First Hand	0672 63163
Informix Software	0784 240444
INMAC Computer Supplies	081 740 9540
Intel	0793 431155
Isles Telecroft	0957 81224
Kodak Diconix	0442 61122
Kompass On-line	0342 326972
Lantastic, Artisoft	0753 554999
LapLink, Traveling Software	0753 818281
Letterkenny ITC, Donegal	(353) 74 24975
Letraset	071 928 7551
Lotus Development U.K.	0784 455445
MacINDEX	081 740 1740
Macromedia	0344 761111
Manchester Host Computer	061 839 4212

Meeting Maker, Frontline	0256 463344
Mercury	0800 424194
Micrografx	091 514 7388
Microplanner	0272 509417
Microsoft	0734 270001
Miracom	0753 811180
MISCO Computer Supplies	0933 400400
Moorlands Telecottage	0298 84336
MultiTech	0344 891266
National Assn. of Teleworkers	0404 47467
NCC for IT	061 228 6333
Network Services Agency	0463 713888
Novell U.K.	0344 860401
Océ	0454 617777
Omnis, Blyth Software	081 346 9999
Pace	0274 532000
Panasonic	0344 853915
Pegasus	0536 411444
Phillips	0800 289800
Pixel Paint, Principal	0706 831831
Powerpoint 3.0, Microsoft	0734 270001
PowerProject, Asta	0844 261700
Quark, Computers Unlimited	081 200 8282
Quarterdeck U.K.	0245 496699
Quicken, Intuit	0800 585058
Racal	0256 763911

Radius	081 200 8282
Reuters	071 251 1122
Roderick Manhattan	071 978 1727
Roland	0252 816181
Rosset Telecottage	0244 571372
RSA Exam Board	0203 470033
Sage	091 202 3000
SCO, Santa Cruz Operation	0923 816344
Sony	0784 67000
Studio 8,16,32, Principal	0706 831831
Sybiz	0635 877777
Symantec	0628 776343
Taxan	0344 484646
The Teleservice Clearing House Ltd	0988 403434
Threadz U.K.	0628 660991
Ventura	0753 550022
Videologic	0923 260511
Word 5.0, Microsoft	0734 270000
WordPerfect U.K.	0932 850500
Wordstar	081 643 8866
WREN Telecottage	0453 834874

Appendix 3

Access Towns and Numbers for the PSS Dialplus Network

A full list of Network Access Points and their telephone numbers is below

GNS Diaplus Connections Access Points operating speeds of 300–2400 bps

Aberdeen	(0224) 210701	Colonsay	(09512) 373
Ayr	(0292) 611822	Crewe	(0270) 588531
Ballymena	(0266) 654284	Dalmally	(08382) 410
Bangor	(0247) 274284	Downpatrick	(0396) 616284
Belfast	(0232) 331284	Dundee	(0382) 22452
Benbecula	(0870) 602657	Dunoon	(0369) 2210
Birmingham	021-633 3474	Edinburgh	041-313 2137
Brechin	(035662) 5782	Elgin	(0343) 543089
Brecon	(0874) 623151	Enniskillen	(0365) 328284
Brighton	(0273) 550045	Exeter	(0392) 421565
Bristol	(0272) 211545	Fionnphort	(06817) 563
Brodick	(077030) 2031	Glasgow	041-204 1722
Cambridge	(0223) 460127	Golspie	(040863) 3021
Canterbury	(0227) 762950	Grimsby	(0472) 353550
Cardiff	(0222) 344184	Guildford	(0483) 38632
Carlisle	(0228) 512621	Halifax	(0422) 349224
Chelmsford	(0245) 491323	Hastings	(0424) 722788
Cheltenham	(0242) 227547	Huntly	(0466) 793653
Coleraine	(0265) 56284	Invergarry	(08093) 406

Inverness	(0453) 711940	Northampton	(0604) 33395
Ipswich	(0473) 210212	Norwich	(0603) 763165
Kings Lyn	(0553) 691090	Nottingham	(0602) 506005
Kingussie	(0540) 661078	Oban	(0631) 63111
Kinross	(0577) 863111	Omagh	(0662) 240284
Kirkwall	(0856) 876004	Oxford	(0865) 798949
Leamington	(0926) 451419	Petersfield	(0730) 265098
Leeds	(0532) 440024	Peterborough	(0733) 555705
Leicester	(0533) 628092	Plymouth	(0752) 603302
Lerwick	(0595) 6211	Poole	(0202) 666461
Lincoln	(0522) 532398	Portadown	(0762) 351284
Liverpool	051-255 0230	Port Ellen	(0496) 2143
Llandrindod Wells	(0597) 825881	Portree	(0478) 3208
Llandudno	(0492) 860500	Preston	(0772) 204405
Locharron	(05202) 598	Reading	(0734) 500722
Lochgilphead	(0546) 603717	Rotherham	(0709) 820402
Lochinver	(05714) 548	Rugeley	(0889) 576610
London, Colindale	081-905 9099	Sedgwick	(0539) 561263
London, Croydon	081-681 5040	Sevenoaks	(0732) 740966
London, Monument	071-283 9123	Shrewsbury	(0743) 231027
London, Clerkenwell	071-490 2200	Southampton	(0703) 634530
Londonderry	(0504) 370284	Stornoway	(0851) 706111
Luton	(0582) 481818	Strathdon	(09756) 51396
Machynlleth	(0654) 703560	Swindon	(0793) 541620
Magherafeit	(0648) 34284	Taunton	(06823) 335667
Mallaig	(0687) 2728	Tobermory	(0688) 2060
Manchester	061-834 5533	Truro	(0872) 223864
Melvich	(06413) 364	Warminster	(0985) 846091
Middlesbrough	(0642) 245464	Wick	(0955) 4537
Mintlaw	(0771) 24560	York	(0904) 625625
Neath	(0639) 641650	Cellnet (V42)	2250
Newcastle	091-261 6858	Cellnet (MC4800)	4800
Newry	(0693) 64284	Vodafone	970970

Network Access Points operating speeds of 9600 bps

Aberdeen	(0224) 211230	Cardiff	(0222) 223871
Belfast	(0232) 241035	Chelmsford	(0245) 347317
Birmingham	021-643 9911	Edinburgh	031-313 3361
Brighton	(0273) 562724	Glasgow	041-221 6442
Bristol	(0272) 294149	Guildford	(0483) 452273

Ipswich	(0473) 288573	Manchester	061-832 4269
Leeds	(0532) 341058	Newcastle	(091) 233 1146
Leicester	(0533) 532983	Nottingham	(0602) 417498
Liverpool	051-236 4057	Plymouth	(0752) 255912
London	081-205 6519	Reading	(0734) 393958
Luton	(0582) 415606	Sheffield	(0742) 757903
Maidstone	(0622) 685447	Southampton	(0703) 339241

The minimum period of service for GNS Dialplus connection is one year

For more information please contact:
GNS Front Office
BT
Network House
Brindley Way
Hemel Hempstead
HP3 3RR
Telephone 0800 282444
9.00 am–5.30 pm, Monday–Friday

Appendix 4

Recommended specifications of different levels of personal computer

Level	Low	Medium	High
Processor/Speed	386SX/25	486SX/25	486DX/66
RAM	2Mb	8Mb	16Mb
CPU Secondary Cache	16Kb	128Kb	256Kb
Bus Standard	ISA	ISA	EISA
Hard Disk Capacity	80Mb	210Mb	340Mb
Video Standard	VGA	SVGA	SVGA
Video RAM	516Kb	1Mb	2Mb
Local Bus	No	Yes	Yes
Windows Accelerator	No	Yes	Yes
Monitor Size	14"	15"	17/20"
Dot Pitch, mm	.31	.28	.26
Expension Slots	4	6	6
Drive Slots	2	4	4
CD-ROM	No	Yes	Yes
Tape Streamer	No	No	Yes

References

1. The Telecommunication-Transportation Trade-off, Nilles Carlson, Gray & Hanneman, Wiley 1976.

2. Tomorrows Workplace – The Managers' Guide to Teleworking, F. Kinsman, B.T.Customer Communications Unit, 1988.

3. Home Sweet Workstation: Homeworking and the Employment Needs of People with Severe Disabilities, Ashok et al, GLC Equal Opportunities Group, London 1985.

4. A Study of the Environmental Impact of Teleworking, B.T. Research Laboratories, Martlesham, 1991.

5. Teleworking – the Human Resource Implications, J & C Stanworth, Institute of Personnel Management, 1991.

6. Office Work in the Home: scenarios and prospects for the 1990s, M Olson, Diebold Group, New York, 1981.

7. Information Technology – The Catalyst for Change, P.A. Consulting Group, W.H.Allen/Mercury Books, 1990.

8. Competitive Strategy, M. Porter, Collier McMillan, 1985.

9. Competitive Advantage – Creating & Sustaining Superior Performance, M. Porter, Collier McMillan, 1985.

10. Information Technology – Social Issues, A Reader, Chapter 7, New Technology & Bank Work, S. Smith & D. Weild, Hodder & Stoughton, 1987.

11. Management Today, Nov. 1991, pp92–93.

12. Management Today, Feb. 1992, p101.

13. Management Today, Sep. 1991, p103.

14. Executive Information Systems, Management Handbook, J. Bird, NCC/ Blackwell, 1991, p23.

15. ACRE, Teleworking Fact Sheet No. 2, 1992.

16. The Moorlands Telecottage Prospectus, S. J. Brooks, Staffordshire County Council, June 1990.

17. Argyll Community Telematics Ltd., The Halfway Report, P. Minshall, ACT 11 Ltd., PO Box 635, Lochgilphead, PA31 8LN, 1992.

18. E.C. Commission, "Future of Rural Society", Supplement 4/88 Bull, E.C. 1988.

19. ORA 1992, R & D on Telematic Systems for Rural Areas, Directorate XIII, Commission of the European Communities, 1992.

20. ORA 1992, Review of current experiences and perspectives for teleworking, Brain & Page Eds., Directorate XIII, Commission of the European Communities, 1992.

21. 1989 Home Office Overview, T. Miller, LINK Resources, New York, USA, 1990.

22. The Telecommuting Resource Guide, Telecommuting Case History May 1985 – July 1989, C. Nolan, Pacific Bell, 1010 Wilshire Boulevard, Los Angeles, CA 91764, USA.

23. Offensive Marketing, J. H. Davidson, 2nd Ed. Penguin Books, 1987, p91.

Bibliography

Executive Information Systems: Management Handbook, J. Bird, NCC/ Blackwell, 1991.

Europe 2002, B. Wahlstrom, Kogan Page, 1991 Home is Where the Office Is, A. Bibby, Headway, 1991. Information Technology, N. Stang, Charles Letts & Co., 1989.

Information Technology: Social Issues, ed. Finnegan, Salaman & Thompson, Hodder & Stoughton, 1987.

Information Technology: The Catalyst for Change, PA Consulting Group, Mercury, 1990.

Local Area Networks, 2nd Ed., M. Devargas, NCC/Blackwell, 1992.

Marketing Today, 2nd Ed., G. Oliver, Prentice-Hall, 1986. Offensive Marketing, 2nd Ed., J. H. Davidson, Penguin, 1987.

Telework, The Human Resource Implications, J & C Stanworth,

Institute of Personnel Management, 1991.

The Complete Guide to working from Home, S. Read, Headline 1992.

The Electronic Office, 2nd Ed., D. Jarrett, Gower, 1984.

The New Realities, P Drucker, Mandarin, 1989.

The Telecommuters, F. Kinsman, John Wiley & Sons, 1987.

Understanding Computers, R. Stevens, O.U.P., 1986.

Glossary

ASCII American Standard Code for Information Interchange, which specifies a standard for the character representation of binary code.

binary A number system based on only two numerals, zero and one.

bit The basic unit of information in a computer, usually represented by a one or a zero.

bps Bits per second

bus The set of electrical connections that carry data from the microprocessor to the memory and the other parts of the computer.

byte A group of eight bits. Each byte is sufficient to store a single character.

CD-ROM Compact Disc, Read Only Memory

CCITT Comité Consultatif International de Téléphonie et de Télégraphie.

clock speed The frequency, expressed in MHz, of the clock crystal pulse that initiates each cycle the microprocessor carries out.

CPU	Central Processing Unit, the core micro-chip of a computer.
DTP	Desk Top Publishing
DOS	Disk Operating System.
daisywheel	A printhead where the characters are embossed at the end of the spokes of a wheel which rotates to bring the required character into the printing position.
digitiser	A device to transfer the co-ordinates of a drawing into digital form which can be recognised by a Computer Aided Design programme.
download	The process of retrieving or copying a computer file from another location.
dot matrix	A printhead where the characters are formed by dots made by a number of pins, usually 9 or 24.
Email	Electronic mail, a means of communication where messages are stored in an electronic mailbox which can only be accessed by the authorised recipient,
EISA	Extended Industry Standard Architecture
file	A block of information stored in the computer; it may be a programme, text or data.
floppy disk	A removable magnetic disk for storing data.
GUI	Graphical User Interface
hard disk	A high density, high speed, magnetic disc for storing data, not normally removable.
hardware	The physical components of a computer such as the microprocessor, disk drives and the monitor.

hexadecimal Refers to the base-16 system of notation in which the digits 0–9 and the letters A–F express the hexadecimal equivalents of the decimal numbers 0–15. If it is not clear whether 0–9 are in hexadecimal form, a prefix "&H" or a suffix "H" is added.

IDE Integrated Drive Electronic, a standard drive interface.

ISDN Integrated Services Digital Network, very high capacity digital telephone lines.

IT Information Technology

icon A pictorial symbol, usually associated with Apple Mac computers or "MS Windows" which represent a programme or procedure. Clicking on the icon will initiate the programme or procedure.

ink-jet A printing technique where the characters are formed by dots of ink from tiny ink guns.

k or kb Thousands of bytes.

LAN Local Area Network

Mainframe A large central computer

Mb Millions of bytes

MCA (a) Micro Channel Architecture, IBM bus standard.

(b) Media Control Architecture, the compatibility standard in the field of Multimedia.

MIPS Millions of Instructions per second

menu A screen layout or a drop down panel within a screen which offers a limited number of procedural choices.

network	Generic name for a number of computer connected to each other in one of a number of ways.
OCR	Optical Character Recognition, a method in which text characters are read by optical pattern recognition.
PTT	A national telephone Company e.g. British Telecom
parallel	In data transmission, a description of the method in which the 8 bits in a byte of data are sent simultaneously along eight separate transmission lines.
Pixel	An individually addressable dot on a monitor screen.
port	The output socket on the back of a computer. They are configured as serial, parallel or sometimes game.
prompt	The on-screen display of the current drive letter, followed by the "greater than" > symbol.
RAM	Random Access Memory
ROM	Read Only Memory
SCSI	Small Computer Systems Interface, an interface standard for disc drives.
scanner	A device which can read text by optical pattern recognition and sends the digital output to an application programme.
serial	In data transmission, a description of the method in which the 8 bits in each byte of data are sent sequentially along a single transmission line.
software	The programmes that control how a computer operates.

Telematics   The integration of Information Technology and Telecommunication Technology.

upload   The process of copying or sending a computer file to another location.

VDU   Visual Display Unit, the computer's monitor or screen.

WAN   Wide Area Network

Index